Knowledge
from the Old

Family Life and Social Issues

Knowledge from the Old

Spiritual Parenting

Benoit Dorsette

KNOWLEDGE FROM THE OLD
SPIRITUAL PARENTING
FAMILY LIFE AND SOCIAL ISSUES

iUniverse books may be ordered through booksellers or by contacting:

iUniverse
1663 Liberty Drive
Bloomington, IN 47403
www.iuniverse.com
1-800-Authors (1-800-288-4677)

ISBN: 978-1-5320-4523-3 (sc)
ISBN: 978-1-5320-4522-6 (e)

Library of Congress Control Number: 2018903634

Print information available on the last page.

iUniverse rev. date: 03/23/2018

Contents

Jacob and Esau, who were they?

THESE TWO MEN WERE TWIN sons of Isaac, Abraham's son, who had them with his wife Rebekah. However, before their birth, Yahweh told Rebekah that two people would be born to her. Two mighty men, leaders of nations, but the older would serve the younger. Although leader of nations, Esau chose to please himself. Like Esau, many people, young and old, have minds that are only on worldly things that perish.

Isaac loved Esau because he was the first born, and wanted him to have the birth right. Isaac made known to his sons what those privileges would be. Young people, I want you to take my advice. Be very careful about what you are going to do with your life, I know that many of you don't pray, but one of the very first things a child should learn from parents is to pray. Fathers you are the heads of your home families, take them to services on Yahweh Sabbath days and so they will learn to read the Bible, even a verse or two per day. Call them in devotion.

Now and then you'll see me using the names Yahweh

and Yahshua in this book. The name of our heavenly father is Yahweh, and his son is Yahshua who died to give life to the world. Yahweh means salvation.

Please read Isaiah 42:8. Parents, please try to establish good things in your children's minds, if you don't the devil will surely give them ideas of what to do and that you'll not like. Fathers as well as mothers should watch their children carefully during their early years. Don't let the chance to learn from them pass just because Esau didn't properly value the blessing while he had the chance to do so. Parents must not uphold improper behaviour or help their children to pursue that which is not good. Don't defend their choices when they are wrong.

And fathers, why do you let your children see your own evil conduct? Make sure to behave properly in front of your young daughters. Mothers, please teach your children to love their fathers, just as you fathers ought to teach your children to love their mothers. I know there are divisions between parents themselves, as well as between parents and their children, but we cannot live like that.

I have noticed that many men are not conducting themselves in a good way; such men are staying in the home most of the time with just an underwear, where there are girls, children in the home. I ask these men to be more careful in the house.

Another evil is that children bearing babies in their parents' home while going to school. Parents, you send your children to school, you do well, but you have to be watchful, finding ways to know about them, even when you are not with them. You send them to school, because you love them and want good for them. But you did not want your daughter or daughters to bring to you a certificate of child bearing. Neither your son or sons. Is there a form of respect in the home when the mother is pregnant at which time that schoolgirl is also bearing? These young girls learn nothing at school because of their carelessness they find themselves in trouble. My question is, are they able to take care of their babies? Please don't get vex with me. I'm just trying to awake you out of bed. Going further, I wish to tell you that some of these young ladies don't even know for whom they are pregnant. So, you parents must be willing to carry the heavy load that they bring from school. The worst part is that some of them carry very little or no respects at all for father or mother, I lie not.

Sometime disagreement comes up between them about this unborn baby, but do you know that no unborn can defend his or herself? It is good that sometimes you allow them to feel their pain but destroy not the innocent. Today men cannot act as they should at home. The father cannot chastise his children or child how he sees it fit to do. He cannot lock the doors when he wants to. He reaches the point that the doors of the house have to remain unlocked at any time for the school girl at 13 years, or for the boy that stays outside at any hour of the night doing what the parents don't know or agree with.

Parents should be able to use the rod of correction when needed. Parents you must train them, go to the book of Hebrews where Paul spoke to the parents, Read chapter 12, verse 5 to 11.

I wish that all who read this book will love what it says.

Is it right that parents should chastise their children or not? Is it right for children to chastise their parents?

I was raised in a very poor home where there was no washing machine, no radio, no television, no walkie talkie, no flushing toilet. My mother could not afford to give me what she would like to give me. She could not afford for herself what she needed, I remember, in a large family we had just one hair comb; she could not give herself a hat for each dress she wore.

She could not afford to buy me a bicycle. Some people had donkeys, I remember a man had a horse, he had also a "humark", but if you don't know what a "hammock" is, what it is made of, what its purpose, let me tell you that a "hammock" was made in those days to carry sick people to the hospital. It was made with a hard "canvice" cutting the "canvice" leaving four holes two on each side.

Four men would carry the hammock. One man on each end. The middle part is hallowed, that's where the sick would be placed. Once used, they would fold it nicely for use again.

In those days one would hardly hear about a hospital. What i am saying is true. Today we have ambulances, we have hospitals, airplanes, all kind of boats, you name them. We didn't know about submarines.

Television of all kinds, and all sizes, we have the cable and internet connections that will help us to get the more. All of these are to make life more comfortable. In years gone by there were not many doctors, not many nurses, not many pharmacies. In those days people were using herbs for medication. Whatever the sickness was they knew what kind of herb to use and that worked out very well.

In years gone by, not to many people had or knew what a bank account was. Banks were not common as we have them today. Most of the people who had a little money to save, would rap it with a piece of plastic nicely, dug a hole in the ground, placed it in the hole and then covered it with dirt. Then planted a flower or any plant over it to mark the place where they hid it. Money was not that easy to have, but the cost of living was not so expensive like it is today. In my childhood days, my mother sent me to buy many times one penny and a half, or penny bread and that would serve for a family of three to four people.

Penny and half soap, penny and a half butter, oil etc. Cooking oil was sold by measure. They would last a week or more. At that time and in those days, we knew nothing about dollars. We used Pounds, Shilling and Pence as our currency. The Euro currency, we had no such dream.

School yes. We were sent to school. Although I did not have a lot of pants and shirts, yet I was sent to school anyway. How well do I remember that? Quite well. I had two school pants and not more than three shirts. I remember that when one set of clothing got dirty, my mother would wash it quickly then squeeze out the extra water. Then she would hang it out in the sun or put it over the stove to dry. But that would happen just as I came from school in the afternoon; because she did not want the two to get dirty at the same time. Food would be cooking, and she would be washing at the same time. As she put off her cooking she would hang that school shirt or pant.

But what kind of stove I'm talking about? Well I'm talking about a three stones stove, maybe you never heard about a three stones stove. The three stones stove is just three stones. The three stones were not placed one on top of another but placed so that dry wood could be placed between each stone. When that is done, they would light a fire in the middle of the stones. When the fire is high enough, she would put her pot on the three stones stove to get her cooking done, so that is the stove I'm talking about.

But what about the pressing of the school clothes that my mother washed? How did she iron or press them? After she washed them and put them to dry over the three stones stove, my mother would have them folded nicely. Put it under her pillow so that while she is sleeping, she would roll over it and that's how the pressing was done so that I could have it to go to school the following day.

Above the three stones stove sometimes when it rained, and the place got cold, the people who used that kind of stove outside were having problems to get the stove lit. Now I do hope that you start seeing the reason for my writing. I must say and I'm glad to have you thinking about the past and to know a little about the past. Now to those who doesn't like the old, I say reject not the old because it is good that the old and young live together. The old are there for many good reasons, believe me.

Were you there, then you would understand better what I'm talking about. The younger ones before were taught to be more respectful towards the elderly.

- ➢ Respect for The Almighty
- ➢ Respect for parents
- ➢ Respect for family members
- ➢ Respect for assemblies
- ➢ Respect for friends
- ➢ Respect for teachers and classmates
- ➢ Respect for enemies
- ➢ Respect for government personnel

That we should also love our neighbours as ourselves. Get wisdom, get knowledge and get understanding.

Parents what role do you play when you see your son or sons, your daughter or daughters falling in what they call Love? Do you take time out to look into such matters? If not, why not?

Please see that you advise them by helping them in making the right choices where getting a life partner is concerned.

By disobeying my mother, I made two bad choices. I once presented a young and beautiful lady to my mother. I thought that my mother would agree when she saw her outward appearance. But, my mother did not agree. However, she couldn't change my mind from dating this beautiful girl.

So, I kept dating this girl for years and then decided to get married. A few years went by, then problems started falling on me. If I was not careful, I could have been in prison. I was asked to divorce her by law. I had a free charge wherein I had nothing to pay to her.

After that one, I took another beautiful one to my

mother. Once again, she disagreed and once again, I held on to my beautiful lady. Out came more problems for me. It would be like I was always going for these beautiful girls.

But what I didn't know is that that the eyes of parents can see further than the eyes of children. My mother gave the reasons why she didn't approve any of these girls, not that she hated them.

After that I saw that I did not obey my mother but disobeyed her. Thinking that I was making the right choices, where as I was not. I knew then that parents often make the right choices in their children's life. Please read ***Exodus 20:12, Proverbs 23: 22-26 and Deuteronomy 5:16***.

Parents before were advising their daughters when finding the one they love not to give in to him, but that they should bring him home, so that the parents would question him, finding from him if indeed he is serious. If serious, he must give a date of marriage.

The girl's parents would find out everything about the boy's family before she would give her daughter to this fellow in marriage. Some children before, when met face to face with their parents about this matter should the parents disagree, they too would disagree and that was for both boys and girls. For this cause, the people before, many of them lasted longer in their married life.

Often times children like to do as they please, and that is not the right way of life. I ask every child, boys or girls to give your father's and mother's the right to guide them in choosing. Many times, the plans the children make brings grief to the parents and to themselves. However, as you go on reading you'll gain the more, but the Bible is the best of all.

Today in the time we live, children are receiving things from parents or from love ones, some of them hardly say a word of thanks in receiving these gifts.

Children must be obedient; how much are you in love with this word obedient? Of course, I know that not many young people obey their parent's rules. But Abraham was one who obeyed the commandments of Yahweh. Proverbs 3; 1-14. Adults also must keep the laws of Yahweh.

Father's laws must stand. Children must learn to obey at all times for it is right, says Yahweh. Deuteronomy 5:16. Esau regarded the law as nothing to give value, but on self-pleasure; only to do his own will. Jacob wanted nothing of what his father had but to have the birth-right to offer sacrifice to Yahweh and that he would receive the blessings from Yahweh. He was always looking forward, not behind. What best do we want in life? He believed that as long as Esau had right as the first born the promise to him could not be gained. Although he studied how he might gain that blessing which his brother regarded lightly.

But one day, Esau came home weary from the field hungry. Jacob was doing some cooking. Esau ask for food to eat. Right away Jacob saw the time had come for him to have what he wanted. He said yes, the food you can get but what about the birth right? Here you will agree with me that when one came from the field, reaching home hungry you will eat whatever you meet, since you are not obeying the laws of Yahweh that speaks about clean and unclean. Leviticus 11:1-47 and also Deuteronomy 14: 1-25.

Esau answered Jacob and said, "I have it. But what good is it to me, when am in the point of death? It profits me nothing, give me food and you can have it."

Salvation should mean more to anyone than gold, silver, sex, money, etc. No one should give away his or her birth right for a dish of red pottage, food. For pleasure will perish but eternal life will be forever.

Had he waited a little longer, he would have gotten food from someone. Here we see that he needed just a little more faith. Rebekah did not have that kind of faith to teach her son Jacob to wait. Yahweh will surely work in his own time. Matthew 4:4, Deuteronomy 8:3.

The weakness here asks that no family should not separate even if there is no money in the home for a while, don't separate from each other. Pray and wait a little longer for this is the time to prove faith in Yahweh. Younger ones, don't go doing things in a hurry, because later on you might regret it. Don't sacrifice the heavenly for the earthly, Moses refuse to have the pleasure of the world. Hebrews 11:24-26.

Many people today still hold on Esau's attitude. Some have come into the assembles of Yahweh. Unable to do as they please, they fall out from the faith. Don't sell your faith for worldly pleasures. Any pleasure apart from Yahweh is worldly. Set your mind on things above and not things of the earth. We don't want to forget Jacob and Esau. The time for Isaac's death was nearing. Old and blind expected to die shortly, he's now looking for ways to pass the blessing to his son Esau. Not knowing that his wife and son Jacob were there to put a stop to his plan. He must do what he has to do. He quickly decided to keep a feast.

Rebekah is looking for ways to win the plan or to stop the plan, but Yahweh will work in his own time. Rebekah may want Jacob to obey her, but when a person is not knowing to do badly, it becomes a problem to start and that was Jacob problem. She said only follow what I'm saying, things will work out. We have to take a chance for it might work. The faster the better. Notice the word "might work". Not definitely, but we must try. Similar to what's said in Genesis 3:1-6

In Genesis Satan told Eve if she ate of the fruit, the forbidden fruit, she might not die. Yahweh's word did not fall in agreement with what Satan said. Yahweh said to the woman that she would surely die if she ate the forbidden fruit. Eve did eat the fruit and gave to her husband and he did eat and death passed on all mankind.

At last Jacob made up his mind. The mother and son won the plan but with problem. Just as Eve ate and brought death. Roman 6:23.

Jacob knows that he had done what was evil against his father. Any wrong advice you give to your children can cause grief to them. Believe me.

Esau said. "Let my father arise to eat what I have prepared for him so that my father can bless me." Then the blind old father now knew that something went wrong but more problems added in his old mind. Esau seek to find it again, but it was too late. Hebrews 12:16-17.

Esau like the people of the world gave very little value for the death of the one who died or who brought salvation to mankind. What will they give when the kingdom is made new on the earth? Many are living their life with no thought or care for the future. They live today like Esau. Many are saying, "let us eat and drink for tomorrow we die." So many still believe that death ends it all. 1 Corinthians 15:32. What is wrong is that they forget or just don't know that there is a judgement after death, did you not know man?

Why not take the best? When one denied self and fear Elohim keeping the commandments of Yahweh, the heavenly blessing will be given. Ecclesiastes 12:13-14. Many times, bad desires take place then Elohim and heaven fails. How many professed believers do things that result in trouble or death, and infect the soul? At which time they should change themselves from unrighteousness of flesh to the spirit. Holiness is perfecting in the fear of Yahweh. They are troubled because they see that they cannot live the way the worldly people live and think to secure their salvation, so they conclude that since the way to archive eternal life is so strict, they rather no longer walk in the right way, Elohim's way.

The age and time in which we live many are selling their birth right for sexual indulgences, sacrificing their lives. They are also sacrificing their health; their faculties mentally enfeeble, and their salvation is cast away just for the "now" pleasure. At the same time, the character is weakening and dying.

Esau awoke to see the mistake he made with his birth right. It was too late to recover what he had lost. Some of those who believe that they are serving Yahweh by doing his will and are not, will go for a surprise. *Matthew 15:7-9; Isaiah 39:13*. Don't sell your salvation for self-gratification; this advice is for men, women, boys and girls.

Remember that multitudes are giving their eternal life for worldly pleasures, such as herbs smoking, partying, sex, drunken driving, etc.

But you alone know what you'll sell your crown for. Will you take a stand for the better?

Have you considered the seriousness of the time in which we live? Have you seen how fast the world is moving? This is not an easy time, but believe me the worst is yet to come.

When I was a child along with other children, our parents would command us what they want of us. Whatever the command was they would see to it that we obey. But now, most parents don't stand behind their own command to their own children. And these children, seeing that their parents are leaving the open hole, take advantage to do as they please.

But no. It could not be so before. The world is in serious trouble. What I hate to hear is that there are some parents who use words like "*let these children enjoy the world to know what the world gives*".

However, my question is. What's in the world anyway? Let me answer that myself. Maybe some of you fathers and mothers, don't have the answer.

Here are some of what's in the world:

➢ *Dirty acts of sex*
➢ *Stealing*

- ➤ *Raping*
- ➤ *Killing for no reason*
- ➤ *Gun shooting*
- ➤ *Adultery*
- ➤ *Fornicating*
- ➤ *Abortion*
- ➤ *Divorcing for any or no cause at all*
- ➤ *Smoking*
- ➤ *People using indecent languages*
- ➤ *No respect from some people*
- ➤ *Lovers of pleasures more than loving Yahweh*
- ➤ *Hating one another*
- ➤ *Back biting,*
- ➤ *Etc.*

These are some fruits of the flesh. These 15 points are just some of which your children will meet as they go further in the world. These and others that you know you should not allow them to get caught up in. Be very careful because if you allowed them to find these in the world, then you parents will cry.

"Still in the world they can find these for good: sports of all kind."

Praying to Elohim first should be going to Yahweh's Sabbath services learning to read the bible. Having respect for everybody, especially for Yahweh and Yahshua, and, to have respect for oneself.

The above points that I made mention of, you should

never as parents let your own kids get into. They will do your kids no good. I remember when I was a child, my mother did not want me following any child that didn't know how to control his or herself respectfully. Much less if she would hear any child saying the word "sex".

Those parents before were very loving. They would give much attention to their kids. If a boy touched a girl's breast, that would cause trouble. Nowadays, boys can do or say whatever they want with the young ladies.

Respect

Our young people seem as though they don't even know what "respect" is. Even some elderly ones as well.

Stealing

Stealing is rampant all around us. In past years, people could leave anything in the open. We were leaving our homes opened many times. Our neighbours also did the same.

No one would come in to steal, everybody was everybody's watchman. *Exodus 20:15, Deuteronomy 5:19, Leviticus 19:11*.

Raping

I hate all the 15 points that are listed here. This one I really don't see eye to eye with, because in today's time, there are so many women. A man should never get involved in raping. What about raping animals? *Leviticus 20:15-16*.

Killing

Some of us know about killing. They kill in wars. Family members kill each other. Often times we hear and see people get killed in our own home town. A person that kills another person is in danger of the commandment of Yahweh. *Deuteronomy 5:17; Exodus 20:13, Matthew 5:21-22*.

Some time ago I heard about a man who killed his own wife. When I heard that I asked myself, "how could that be?" I ask a friend, "how could a man kill his wife?" The friend told me in reply that it's a matter of love. My other question was what kind of love is that? The friend goes on to say, many times when these women go away form their husband, in other words when they decide not to be with their husband anymore, they go on to another man, doing all in their power to rundown their husband, making the man feel that he is the boss.

The big problem is that the husband still desires to have his wife. But in cases like this, the man who have this man's wife feels that he is the big macho man. So, he does things with the woman that creates jealousy to the husband and that form of jealousy by the husband can create a fight which can cause the wife's death. My advice on that point is to avoid fornication. Let each woman have her own husband. Let the husband render to the wife her due and likewise also the wife to the husband. Again, I would like to ask. Is it not better for the man to leave that man's wife than to stay with her until she's killed, especially knowing that the husband still wants or loves his wife? The case with the women is the same question. Don't stay with her because of you, she might lose her life. But remember you too oh man, can be killed.

Leaving her husband: When a wife leaves her husband for another man, things always look good in the beginning, but in process of time things does change between them. But then, only then, regretful thoughts begin to come in. Then what's next? I remember knowing a man and his wife. One day, this man happened to call a fellow man name to his wife while they were in a disagreement. He called the fellow man name because it was said to him that this same fellow man was having some interference with his wife.

What was the wife response? The response from the wife to the husband was that the fellow man has prepared himself for anyone who tells him anything about having a man wife. Then the husband asks the wife, "how is he preparing?" She replied to her husband that the fellow man has a bag full of guns, and the guns carry big bullets. Then the husband who understands his wife quite well, answered and said; "are you not ashamed to say that to your husband?"

A woman needs to be polite and know how to answer the man in the family. Be it husband, or boyfriend, because some men are very impolite and will not agree with an answer like this especially concerning another man.

As I told you before I know the husband very well, he is a good man, but remember all men are not the same.

Adultery: Adultery is a sin against one self, and it's against Yahweh. In **Deuteronomy 5:18, Exodus 20:14, Leviticus 20:10, 1Corinthians 6:15-20.**

Sex before marriage is sin, for there is no licence for sex until marriage takes place.

Abortion: What could be more dangerous than for a mother to kill her unborn baby? But why have an abortion? Is it because the woman involved herself with another man, finding herself in trouble and not wanting her husband to know, not wanting her religion to know, not wanting her parents to know, not wanting those who goes to school together with her to know, is it the man who did the job not wanting the responsibility? Why should one do that?

All of these are points that I am showing, that some women use to justify their guilt. I am not trying to talk badly about anyone. I am saying that which is happening right in our very eyes, so don't get mad with me.

Divorcement. To divorce for any cause is out of it. The only reason for it is if one is caught in the act of adultery.

Matthew 19:1-12

I am trying my very best to enlighten you. I wrote this book by experience. It is my pleasure to have you in remembrance because many of what I say you truly know. To say more about divorce I personally don't see nothing between a man and his wife that should cause a separation because to me there is nothing that a man or a woman can do to each other that cannot be forgiven. Please read **Matthew 19:1-12** again.

To many people think that a divorce will make the problem lighter. Most of the time it gets worse. Leave out the stubbornness, leave out that little hatred, be willing to communicate with each other, be willing to forgive each other. **Matthew 18:21-35, Mark 10:2-12.**

Communicating and forgiving is the two main points to keep a happy family. Without these acts there are no sure assurance that it will last.

Standing

At one time the two were standing before a priest, a pastor, or an elder. There the one, be it the priest, be it the elder, or the pastor read the wedding ceremony. He pointed out all the pledges. The man and the woman agreed and became husband and wife. They were both happy and rejoicing. They kissed each other in love.

But now there is no money in the home. One wants a divorce. One is older than the other. One is seeing someone else.

Or Is it because wealth increased?

Say whatever you will, but none of the above points are valid for that which one is asking.

We reach an age that the husband cannot even advice his wife in the style of dressing. The wife also wants to give her husband some good advice but is unable to because the man feels that he is the man, and that he needs no advice from his wife.

Listen women. No good husband will agree for his wife

to dress half naked leaving his house. That can create a problem and if not handled properly, can cause the one to ask for a divorce.

However, this is one of the unvalued reason.

What makes the deference between a priest, pastor, an elder, a judge, a lawyer in the case of seeking a divorce? Permit me to answer that myself. The big difference is this. The three joins the two together, but the two, the judge and the lawyer puts the separation between the man and his wife.

It seems to me that the one who is asking for the divorce has forgotten those vows they made and agreed to walk in. Don't try to damage yourself. Remember you are the one who agreed to get married. Don't do like some who threw away their wedding ring. Remember at one time how excited you were to receive that wedding ring.

Those who were once married and did not keep up with it has no say in another person's marriage. Be it man or women. In my young days, one of the biggest shame was for a married couple to separate. It was so shameful that the couple's children would carry the shame. These two people who destroyed their married life as I said should never be invited in another couple's marriage because I am afraid. Should they get to call themselves friend of the bride and friend of the bridegroom, they can damage these two also in their marriage. I want you to go back and read **Matthew 19:1-12**

Drugs

Taking Drugs: It seems very clearly to me that when people take drugs and overdose themselves, they become not the same as they were before. They act differently. Some of them can be very dangerous both to themselves and to others. Many changes take place in their lives.

Indecent languages: Our generation. This new generation will do and say anything. They give respect to nobody, and they can even curse their parents. Have you taken a good look at this generation lately? Well go back and look again. Maybe to you it is something nice, but listen to what the bible has to say about this generation. Read **Proverbs 30:11-14, Isaiah 59:1-8, Psalm 78:8, Deuteronomy 27:16, Proverbs 2:15, Proverbs 4:24-27, Proverbs 4:10-23, Proverbs 12:19-23, Romans4:3, 1Corinthians 10:1-11.** These are just a few texts that point to the attitude of this generation. Lots more can be found in the bible.

The Tongue: It is a very small member of the body. Not tamed properly can create great problem to the owner. We should be very careful how, where, when, for what causes we use our tongue. Never forget when using this little member of the body, that the giver of life is there near to you.

Respect: Since some people can do as they please, it does not matter how others feel or think, they go on doing what they want to do. They go on saying what they want to say, no matter who hears, or sees them. Be it priest, elder, mother and father, they don't care. They'll go on pleasing their own self. They have no respect for the aged ones.

Lovers and pleasures more than lovers of Yahweh: They mind earthly things. For example, when the Christmas holiday comes these people can be seen very busy. They spend lavishly throwing things outside, bringing in new things inside, feasting all over the place, drinking and driving without limit, cursing one another, even fighting one another. Whereas, when Yahweh's feast days comes, just a faithful few will attend.

Leviticus 23:1-44 will prove to you that Christmas is not mentioned and cannot be found anywhere in the bible.

Carnival, this pagan festival carried in some places. Days even weeks. At time, you'll find or meet with many people. Men, women, boys and girls. Many are jumping up while others are standing watching. Some are changing their look and style. Their attitude and behaviour are not in harmony with Yahweh. At carnival, the people are eating, drinking, smoking anything they desire. It is not a clean festival because while they are eating, drinking, and smoking they are robbing on each other in a very disorderly manner.

What good does one find in carnival? Why let your little ones participate in carnival? Yahweh is calling his special people to be different, please read **John 2:15-17**. What is the meaning of carnival, a period of feasting and reverie just before length including "Mardi gras" or "Fat Tuesday", it is a merry making, and mean flesh farewell.

A true converted person should not take part in carnival.

Hating And Backbiting

These two are very common in some people mind. Those who are feeding these habits should try their very best to eliminate them from their minds. Don't follow the system for it is not clean. It is very corrupted **1John 2:9-11.**

A Better Life

REALLY TALKING ABOUT A BETTER life in the now I can understand because we have all kind of facilities, which there were not before. If you remember I talked about the three stones stove. Now should I go using that form of stove it would be like many would say he cannot even buy himself a stove? For so it is now people don't want to stay behind but pushing to go forward.

Before the fifties and sixties people were living far better than now with each other. Let me give you just one point for example. In those days, my mother and my neighbour got into a disagreement. I should never pass by my neighbour who is having the disagreement with my mother and not say hello. This same neighbour, should I have winked my eyes at her, or looked at her in away way not respectful, would give me a spanking and send me home. When I arrived home, I dare not tell my mother because if she is not pleased with what I did, it was possible for me to get another spanking from her.

The education back then was that when older folks

got into their misunderstanding, children should not get involved. Now in the time we are living, it's not the same. Any problem between neighbours and children of both parties are having their opinion. Even taking the problem in hand.

Children were taught to greet the elderly. If they were receiving anything, they were to say thank you sir, or thank you miss. I was taught to say "howdy" (How do you do) to anyone as often as I met with the same person. When a child would do that which was wrong, for example passing between two adults, one of these two had the right to spank that child and send him or her home.

What I want you to understand is this. In those days it was not only the parents raising their children. Any adult would teach a child how to carry on with respect. Parents before didn't want their children to be rude.

Where did such good times go? Can we find it and bring it back? I hardly believe that. Nowadays, most parents will say, nobody should touch my child, nobody should spank my child, no one is helping to feed my child, nobody have nothing to say to my child.

They are saying that in front of those children and this is how it is now. Those fathers and mothers acting in that form of way always believe that they love their children. But no. You don't love them at all believe me. You just making life worst for your kids.

My child is in school, who is in charge? Parents from the time you bring you kids to school, and you turn your back the teacher or teachers are responsible. To teach and to correct. To correct in any way, they saw fit. They are in charge. Their eyes, their ears are open towards that child.

If that child behaviour is not good, the teacher has all rights to admonish the child. According to what the child is doing I would agree with the teacher even to spank that child. Not for any cause but for a good cause, spanking should be used. I expect that you father and mother should live with that. *Proverbs 22:1-6*

If abuse takes place, you the parents have full right to see about that with the teacher in a meek and humble manner to settle it in peace. That's my advice to you parents. Please don't close the door of learning on your children.

Leave the door of mercy open to them.

Let me tell you a little something. What one eats that's what get you upset, and what gets you upset that's what you'll vomit believe me.

I say that because I'm seeing some young people having children and the way they conduct themselves it's very shameful. Then you join me by saying how they live their life so will they raise their kids. Then there is no way that this system can ever get better, but worse.

How were children sleeping before? The boys and girls were sleeping together on the same bed. But from the time the girl or girls started to grow Breast, the parents would separate them. The boys were given their own bed likewise the girls. Say what you will, we had good training before. The life setting before was better than what we have now. It was better in many ways and safer. A well trained up life for children.

Many times, we blame the children for not having

respect, but some adults don't know anything about respect. There are things that an adult should not do while in the home. A man in the home should not use indecent languages, he should not fight the woman in the home, he should not always come home late, he should not smoke, he should not dress as a vagabond, he should not even drink alcohol, he must not stay in the house with just an underwear. He should always knock before entering the girls room.

My Daughter Is on The Stage

WHEN A FATHER KNOWS THAT his daughter is dancing on the stage, dancing and whining especially if she wears a dress in a nude manner, he should never go watching. In the first place she should never be there. Fathers should always stand for principle, the good one; stand as a man.

Some of our young ones are allowing their hands to go too far in touching things which does not belong to them. There are times when fathers and mothers know the evil that their kids are doing and doing nothing to stop the bad that their children are doing. **Proverbs 2:1-22, Proverbs 8:1-11.**

It would be good, very good if we could go back to the old days and take our children with us, where unity and love were better. And then and only then, by the help of Yahweh the almighty, we would be having less problems in this world.

The younger ones are watching the lifestyle of the older ones. For this cause we as older ones should not misconduct ourselves and say that there might be better hope for our young ones. It is a very poor chance. Like that married woman that I talked about earlier about the husband calling another fellow man's name.

The woman did not carry any form of respect to her husband. She in the dispute insulted her husband again. She repeated so many insulting words to her husband about his mother. Each time she used indecent languages, the husband would ask her not to do it, but she would continue in a worse way.

There were four girl children hearing these indecent words, hearing their father asking their mother not to use these bad words. At last the husband shed tears. At the end the smallest girl rebuked her mother for her action. But children raising up, seeing their father and mother behaving in such a rude way will do them no good. And such lifestyle can damage their little mind.

Is there not a better picture to hang on the wall than for married people to conduct themselves like that? I wish never to disrespect my mother in law, both men and women should at all times respect their mother in law.

When a mother will treat the man she loves well, she is opening the gates of love for her daughters; she will learn how she should treat the man in her life. The fathers also should do the same with their sons. When problems arise between a husband and wife, they must never get their children involved. They must handle it between themselves. Close the bedroom door then find the way to solve the problem. The kids should not see daddy vex with mummy, and mummy vex with daddy. Be very careful.

There are many ways to handle the problem not

allowing the children to be there. You can send them to sleep, or let them go and play, or send them to the shop etc. Don't discuss your problem on the road in front of the children. You should always be pleasant.

If you will understand, understand what is written here is to help you to know how it was before and how it is now. It is like those that have ears to hear let them hear, and those that have eyes to see let them see.

Let me tell you ladies a little something. When you notice that trouble is about to take place between you and your lover, first pray, and then go to him and give him a nice kiss, hug him up, because men like their ladies to hug and kiss them. Not to fertilize the problem, but cool it down.

When you try your best to solve a problem even if you don't get it solve don't give up. Remain silent. Don't turn your back and walk away from him. Doing that will do no good. Or You can go to your bedroom, close the door, call him in and kiss him again trying still to get ways to calm him down. I believe that this time you are sure to get a good result from his angered rage.

Be wise, be smart, knowing that you as a woman, having him to know that he has but the best woman, and when the question is asked, where can a good woman and worthy be found? He can say quietly in reply I know one, and even know where she can be found, what about that? **Proverbs 31:10-31.**

What About Adam?

YAHWEH MADE THE CREATION WITH all kinds of things in the earth, under the earth, the sea and everything therein. He made man last. Yet everything was placed into the hands of man. Man was the one who named the animals. He called them by their names, whatever he called them that were their names. He, Adam was to keep and to dress the garden, the paradise, a nice and beautiful place, fruits, animals, etc. But there was nothing to look like him there. A lonely man needing someone by his side. Yahweh saw that and promised to give him someone, a help meets, one suitable for him, a woman. So, an operation took place. Yahweh put the man to sleep, took a rib from him, forming into a woman. When the man awoke, there was the gift for the man. Yahweh asked Adam what do you call it? A woman, he said. What name you give to her? I call her Eve.

The man was not made to be alone, he was to be a happy man. The creation was to be a place of joy and happiness. Had the man stayed alone, the garden would not be the glorious place it should be.

Elohim Gave

WITH THIS WOMAN THE MAN would be communicating. A companion suited for him. He would not be controlled by her since he was made to be the head. But to be comforted by her company. He Adam, was not made to use extra force over her. She was to receive protection from him. What a beautiful picture Yahweh created. She was a part of the man's bone, flesh of the man. This operation should cause a strong tie between the man Adam and his wife Eve. For no man was made to hate his own flesh, but to take care of himself. Ephesian 5: 22-33. The bible goes on to say therefore shall a man leave his father and mother, and shall cleave to his wife. And they the two, the man and the woman shall become one flesh. Why do married people forget that? It is just because there is no fear of Elohim in them. Yahweh never gives to man that which is bad, but always good. The time limit in marriage is death. When Elohim planted the garden, everything was beautiful.

And everything was good. Nothing seemed wanting to meet the happiness of the man and his wife, Adam and

Eve, a Holy pair. So why ask for divorce then? The people don't fear Elohim.

Too many married people are breaking or falling apart for nothing. The wife will say that the husband has another woman; the husband will say the wife doesn't want to sleep with him. Accusing each other falsely will cause a problem between a man and his wife, so no one should do that to each other.

Ephesians 5: 22-33.

There is no law preventing a wife from talking to another man. She can talk to whomever she wants, but she must remember at all time that she has a husband. Therefore, she must limit her conversation. What about the husband? Can he do anything with other women? He must remember at all times that he has a wife. So, he must also watch his conversation.

Both man and woman must be very intelligent if they want their married life to be successful. Intelligent enough to know when someone is bringing a false news or a complain that will in no way make the marriage stronger.

I know about a man having one or two daughters driving around with him sometimes. But while doing that, there are people seeing them sitting by their father. Not knowing that they are father and daughter, somebody carried false news to the man's wife, told her that her husband is always driving and having other women sitting close to him. The wife took the news wrongly and that created a big problem between them.

Women especially should not give these people place in their home. Don't regard them as friends. Tell your husband about what they said so he can fix the matter with them or just tell them that your husband doesn't like people carrying news about him. I bet you that you will never see them again. Don't worry to call them your best or good friends. They are your worst friends. Man, you must also watch the news reporters, don't go damaging your good relationship at home.

When a man sees his wife keeping too close a friendship with another man, he has his full right to stop his wife. However, when he takes the stand to prevent her from going closer, the wife should be glad to have a man who is able to get her out of trouble. She should not think to say to her husband to leave her alone and not to bother her because she is a big woman and not a child.

Not paying attention to what the angel said, Eve soon found herself looking with admiration upon the tree that Yahweh warned her from. We can say the same thing. Some men ask their wife to be mindful to caution. But the other way around, they will soon find themselves involved with some other men. But here I say that both men and women, if not careful can get themselves in big trouble.

The fruit was very beautiful, Eve questioned herself. Why did Elohim withhold it from them? No loving father has the right to let his children or child get into trouble without giving a warning. The loving husband will do the same for his darling wife. Any woman finding herself in trouble with another man should seek help from her husband. Mrs Adam should have sought help from her husband. The tempted opportunity was that as if he was able to discern what was on her mind, knowing that the woman had no strength by herself.

Satan addressed her. Eve, yea hath Elohim said you should not eat of every tree of the garden? Now she sees trouble. Eve was surprised as she seemed to hear the same thing ringing her thoughts, but the serpent did not stop. He kept that musical voice. That's why I said that a woman ought to be very careful when there is another man after her, for the more she listens to that man, coming closer to him she will find something that attracts her mind, then big trouble for her.

When the serpent saw that she is paying attention to him, he kept on telling her what she likes to hear. Instead of fleeing from that wicked serpent, she stayed there wondering. Had she forgotten that she has a husband? My good ladies, don't forget the one you love, don't you put off your mind to listen to what other men have to say to you, and don't you linger to hear what this other man have to offer. Outside, in this world, there's nothing better than what you already have inside. Remember that while you stay lingering he is inside wondering what has become of you and where you could be.

Eve was addressed by an Angel. She could get excited by her thoughts, but the woman Eve had never thought that the evil serpent, man's worst enemy would cause her fall; both for her and all mankind. As I always hear them say, "keep playing with fire and you'll get hurt or burn."

Men having other women apart from the one at home are also in danger. This or these women can cause that good relationship between one man and one woman to sink, breaking the two apart, getting that good happiness to be destroyed.

It is my desire to call on all those who have the rule over us, the preachers, to those who make plans, to pastors, elders, priest, judges, lawyers, teachers, etc, to look into the laws of marriage more seriously to see if it is better to break up or to rebuild a family when there is just a little problem or no problem at all.

It can be seen all around us today that the man or the woman when wanting to do their own thing can pay thousands of dollars to get a divorce. But when that is done, they don't only destroy their life, but also destroy the life of the little ones they left behind. It would be better if there could be a solution to fix than to separate them from each other.

So many people are seeking divorce. Would it not be better before giving the divorce, that the judge or lawyer takes these people to counselling? I have a problem with this and think that these people are doing it for a style. It is possible to restore them together for there is hope for tomorrow.

Matthew 19: 3-11. Get the spirit of forgiving, don't you block the love doors with your foolishness, go back or stay home and fix the small problem that you have.

Is There a Man?

WHERE ARE THE FATHERS AND the mothers? Too many children are independent, what's the reason? Fathers and mothers should try their true best to bring or raise their offspring in the good way. No child should say that he loves his father and he's on his side, or should any child say I love my mother, but I hate my father. But should love their parents.

Remember that one day the Judge and lawyer in heaven will question you about these children and you better don't find yourselves guilty.

Dressing How?

It's the duties of the fathers and mothers to show their children how they ought to dress. The boys and girls alike. The boys having three or four pants on them at the same time is not good. Pants that are falling under their buttocks. They having to be pulling up the pant to be able to walk is not a good sign of respect. No respect at all for you parents.

The girls are having their bodies showing off and walking half naked. It's indecent, not a good sign for a young woman, and it's untidy. That's not how a lady should dress. These young stars will puff their weed as they wish, no one can stop them. They can come home at any time they choose to, no one to stop them.

They use indecent languages at all time, anywhere. They have no fear of Elohim, no fear of their parents, no fear of anybody. They don't want to do anything at home, or around the house. All they want is to come home to eat, drink, take their bath, sleep and wake up. The girls can sit the whole day in front of the television and that is no problem for her. She can smoke a marijuana joint if she wants who cares? She doesn't have to do no cooking, no scrubbing in the home; whose business? She doesn't worry what father or mother will say. She doesn't have to come home; she can stay all night out as long as mother knows, daddy doesn't have to know, that's his business!

And those are just some of the things happening in the home between parents and their children. However, these habits should not be tolerated.

Find The Way

THE NEW ROAD OF LIFE is what many people are looking to travel on because this new way of life can lead them faster to where they are going. But how many people know to themselves that this new road of life is not safe? There's grave danger when travelling on this new way of life.

Let us go back on the old road of life. The little road, the old little road and take our little ones with us. The slower we may drive or walk, safety is there to find.

Our First Parent

OUR FIRST PARENTS WERE NOT left without direction and warning about what would happen, in the garden. There were two maps, one leading to life, and the other leading to death. Satan had a plot to advise the woman wrongly. That is why Elohim said not to eat, nor touch. No laws were placed on the animals except when directed by their owners. The man should never forget those laws because he will be brought to judgement because he was responsible. Yahweh let the man have the whole creation in charge. Yahweh gave man understanding to know what he wants from man. That he must be obedient to his laws. But by judging wrong we find that guilty are set free, while innocent is paralysed.

Eli And His Sons

WHO WAS ELI? HE WAS a ruler in Israel. His responsibility was great. Yahweh called him to be a priest and that the people would look on him for guidance. He was to give also his household orders. He had authority over the nation, yet with all that he had his eyes close. You know sometimes one can be too easy to be a leader. Yahweh expected that he, Eli would control his household with perfect order, but he closed his eyes not minding the sins that his sons are committing. He allowed his sons to do what they wish. He did not take his power in hand to correct the evil habits of his children. He allowed them to even disobey Yahweh. Are we not in an age like this? Yes. We are. Are we not seeing the Eli attitude? Yes. We are. One of the father's strong responsibility is to see about his children education. Education in all form.

And that's when he failed. He went carelessly with the nation and so with his house hold. Like him many rulers fail the nation that they rule. We have plenty fathers today like this. Many parents in the time we live fail to take a firm stand when it's in their right to do so. Treating the matters too lightly. Men that are moving away from duty when they should stand behind their responsibilities, I call them cowards. Eli left his children to do what they wanted, and failed to fit them for service of Yahweh.

Elohim Said

YAHWEH KNOWS ALL HIS PEOPLE, and that is the reason why he said, I know him meaning Abraham that he will command his children and his house hold after him. They shall keep the laws of Elohim and the duties of life, of justice and judgement. Genesis 18:19, Psalm 41:2-5. That was not said about Eli, because he was weak. We have a lot of Eli type today. The fathers become subject to the children. As I said already, when children are left by themselves, they can bring shame to their parents and to themselves. They regarded Yahweh's laws as nothing. They were accustomed to the service of Yahweh. Their character pattern was not proper. They had no rule over them. Although from childhood, they were trained in this matter. Instead of coming more holy, they became weaker. They gave their father no respect in this matter.

So there comes a time when rebellion take place. They were in a very good class with Yahweh, but these wicked men carried their disregard into the service of Elohim. Instead the sons of Eli didn't carry Yahweh's service. They only thought how they could make a mess of it. There was a time when Eli was mad in that he did not stand enough behind his sons so that they should minister in the holy office by allowing his sons from one fault to another, he became blinded to their guilt of sin. But at last they met their stop at which time he could no longer close his eyes from their evil doings. Because the people saw and reported the wickedness of his sons. He was then distressed. They saw their father's daughters but still not in their minds to make a change. Had the priest Eli dealt with his wicked sons, they could have been put off from the priestly office, while their punishment would bring them death. Death would gain victory over them.

Parents, I would like you to know and take interest in what is written here. Open your minds, and do to your children everything that is good, both for now and here and after, if you love them deal with them as your children, but don't you agree one bit with their evil doing.

Remember that when the Judge of Israel failed to carry his work, Elohim took the matter into his own hands.

Question To Eli

DID A MAN FROM YAHWEH come to Eli and say to him, thus said Yahweh, did I plainly appear unto the house of thy father when they were in Egypt in pharaoh's house? And did I not choose him out of all the tribes of Israel to be priest to me to offer upon mine alter to burn incense, to wear an ephod before me? And give into the house of thy father all the offering made by fire to the children of Israel? Therefore, kick ye at my sacrifice and at mine offering which I gave order in my dwelling place and honoured thy sons above me to make thyself fat with the chiefest of the offerings of Israel my people? For this cause, the Elohim of Israel saith, and said indeed that the house and the house of your father should walk before me forever.

The Almighty says in his word, be it far from me, for them that honour me will i honour, and them that despise me shall be lightly esteemed.

Eli Household

ELI DID NOT PUT IN order his household in the way Yahweh wanted, according to Yahweh's rules for families. He followed his own judgement, the fond fathers over looked. The faults and sins that his sons practiced in their youth days they got and had privileges to do as they pleased, thinking to himself that after a time they would handle their habits rightly.

Those parents, fathers and mothers who think that they can give rights to their kids to do as they please one year and the second year they'll get them to stop, are out for a big mistake believe me. All children must be corrected at the right time, and the home must be to them the first best school. If any of you give way to your child, to do as they wish, both you and Eli are the same in this wickedness.

My friends read and do what it says and let your little ones learn to do the same, read **Proverbs 24, 20-25.** Train them well when they are not going the right way, but you must be ready at all times to give to them your home principles and good morals.

Proverbs 22:6, Proverbs 23:19-26, Proverbs 23:15-17.
Don't think that you are wiser than Yahweh, and your ways
in training your kids is the best way. Teach them the ways
of Yahweh.

I have heard people say that their children are still
small to be corrected and to be punished give them some
more chances, wait until they become older, and can be
reasoned with. However, when one waits long to salt the
meat, it got spoiled and then to be thrown away. The wrong
habits if not put off will stay until they meet second nature,
these children will grow up without the proper strictness
of life.

One of the greatest curses in a family is to let the youth
love their own way. Be very willing to raise your children
differently from those we see on the road going wild. Let
the husband and wife stay together in bringing up their
children. There are some that are very bad when training a
child. The mother must not stop the father from correcting
the children. Don't you push the mother aside thinking the
job will be well done by only you.

When the father will not agree for the mother to correct
her child or children it's a sign of weakness from the father,
you two must be in unity. Good unity to do a good job.
Many time dads leave the job for the mother even if he is
there or not. There are times when you men should sit and
watch their behaviour, i mean the form of respect they give
to their mothers, if not pleasing to her sir, you should now
take over the matter in hand. This cooperation between
the man and the woman will eventually get children to act
differently. Try that and see.

The now life style is asking parents to be more loving, more careful, more serious, not supporting them in any evil you see, helping them to be men and women for tomorrow. When these are done they'll be having respect for you and for everybody.

The life style of the now children has spread all over the world, and Satan has held them captive to do his will. That evil seed will affect families, governments and communities; when youths adopt bad habits, while their parents are professing the truth about Yahweh, has brought reproach in the world.

Today's Style

YEARS AGO, THE WOMEN DID not know anything such as is called protection or prevention. In other words, anything that could be used as to prevent a woman from having babies. I cannot remember hearing such thing as i am hearing now, no not at all.

It was not the habits of those women before when they find themselves carrying a baby for the man they love to destroy it. They would carry it. When the baby is born, they would do whatever they could to bring up this child. Sometimes it was hard with them, like my mother who made 13 children. However, with good training, with good principle, and with good morals they brought us up. Some children became doctors, some became policemen, some became fishermen, and some became lawyers, good men and women, Pastors, elders, Priest etc ... Although times were hard with them. Of course, I can say that, some did fail in life. But those that failed, it was not because of their parents' fault. I knew of some who had 15 children. It was not in their minds to do away with any but carry them how they could.

There are men who think that the woman in the house is their servants. No sir. She is not your servant. You must help her sometimes in whatever work she has to do in the house. Be that kind of man. I'm not sending women to have fifteen children. All I'm saying is not to destroy the seed that is sworn in you.

I do agree with any woman, if while bearing that baby, there is problem between life and death, the doctor sees it fit to take it out to save her life, yes; let it be.

Those poor women before, many of them did not have what most of our ladies have today. The facilities that the women today have. They did not even dream about. Not too many of them could afford a small cradle. So where were they putting their babies to sleep you may ask.

Well my answer to your question is simple. A very common thing it was for them. They were having their babies on the house floor in a safe place. They were using old used cloth, or we would call them old rags. At the same time the mothers could have their baby in their arms to sleep.

I have seen that the system that we are now dealing with is one that brings to us problem after problem. School problem in the playfield, problem on the streets, problem all over. Not forgetting it's problem between islands, from one nation to another. But the worse is when there is a problem between family members.

Husband and wife should love to pray to Yahweh in Yahshua's name seeking for guidance.

Don't go out with bad friends. Remember he whom you love will be looking for you, don't let him meet you in the dancing hall; don't let her meet you sleeping by another woman when you gave her the small sum of the money you got.

Husband and wife, father and mother, it's better to stay at home, read and study the bible with the family than to follow the old system. It is better and will strengthen them in love. Many men when wanting a woman to marry before would seek her out from a certain religion for these women could be trusted. Saving money together were the doing of those many husbands and wives, they knew that they were one, and that money should not separate them. There were no secrets between them, they knew their duties to each other. Would you believe me if I told you that before, many of those good women, when their lover especially the husband goes to the field, to the garden to do a day's work, knowing he is about to come home, would ask a child to get ready some water. As soon as he arrived home, would wash himself, or do his self-cleaning. Sometime the mother or the wife would get the water ready. I don't know if that still exist today.

The man that knows his rule to play will be at home to guide his family but others at home must let him do the guiding. He should protect his family from evil. When there were problems between a family in time past, they would seek to find where it came from, who caused it, looking for solution to solve it, not letting it rule the home. The bible speaks about letting no one put a sunder, that is to the two-married people. The man and the woman. Not the man with man and woman with woman. Let not the man nor the woman put a sunder, but stay and try to work out that little problem before it gets worse. I heard women say while having problem at home, that they would not leave their children and go away. They had their sorrows to share, like it is now, but those holy women would not use that as a stamp to run away.

Our Time Is Now

IF PEOPLE WHEN HAVING PROBLEM with others, would seek to find ways to solve the problem, I fully believe that they would find a way. Don't feed hatred in yourself. Seek peace between you and those you are at war with.

Pride Between

SINCE THERE IS PROBLEM AT home that is too heavy to handle, the man feels that one of the way he might get it solved is to go away for a little while. Leaving the wife or the woman at home, he hopes that while away, she will think and question herself. But first, she has to find him to bring him back. If she does that, it is a sure sign that she is a good woman, and does not like what is going on. But if while he goes, she doesn't care about him and the problem because pride within her. When he returns home he might still meet the problem there. No problem comes by itself. But when it comes, we must be ready to find ways to get away from it. There are problems that cannot be solved easily. But if one is looking for a way to get out from it especially in families, and the other is not, then the problem becomes harder. A good man should always see himself trying, even if he has to say sorry many times. You, lady should try, even if you have to give up your rights, don't let the devil tell you that you cannot get it solved.

Letting others know when there's problem at home, one

ought to be very careful how to deal with it and to whom we tell our problem. There are times the woman when seeking ways to get out from the trouble, goes to the wrong set of people. She feels that her friend or friends must know. So, lady O, she takes her sorrows to her friend. She explains to her friend lady B what is going on. Sometimes she is right in what she says, or she might not be right. Her friend will listen to all she has to say. Her friend lady B gives her advice and tells her to try and fix the problem and that she'll pray for her. Now lady O, doesn't agree to the answer she got from lady B. So, she takes her problem, that little misunderstanding to her sister Q. So, she says to Q. "I alone who knows what I'm going through I can't stand it any longer." What answer do you think that lady Q gave her? The answer she lady O was looking for. And that is, Q swells up and says to her. It's you alone that can stand this. If I was in your place, I know what I would do. So, she asks Q what would you do? Q gave a swell up face and said, I would kick him out and take someone else.

Remember I'm trying to show you as a people how you can handle the problem or problems that are confronting you. I use this example about a lady taking her problem to her friend. There I did not use a man because men, if at all hardly do it that way. When under problem others might see him sad or he might go drinking the more. We all know how men stay. If he has a problem on his job, he might easily tell it to his friends.

So too often we let the system rule us when we ought to rule the system. Let us as people, having understanding, don't carry a size of shoes that is too big for us. For if we do our offspring's might do likewise and we may not like to see them. Don't open bad roads, but good roads; let us lay good foundation that our children can build on. Foundation on solid rock not on sinking sand. Sometimes one may carry her problem to a so called good friend, think that she is doing something good. Yes, that friend might show you that she is with you in your sorrows but deep down in her heart she might be very glad, and that you cannot know. You should be very careful. Think on the problem and help him to get it solved. Sir, you also must help her to get it solved for your own good.

When a home is broken, the street people take that in hand and make it worse. They laugh at the family. Some stand for the woman, some for the man. Often, they look at those kids as nothing, and it was for such reason those holy women before would stay home to work out their problem. Some people make those children look so uncomfortable, even to mock them; gossip about them causing them to have tears in their eyes. Both man and woman should see to have the beneficence of the heavenly father. Let the home be full of sunshine and this will be worth far more to you and to your children than land or money. The bible talks about a woman brought before Yahshua, it was because she the woman was caught in the very act of adultery. The bible says that she was forgiven and sent not to be caught in that same act again. If any is found in adultery, try to see if things could work out and not to do it again.

Before we act we must think. Especially when we have children. Or else the decisions we make, can cause harm to those children. A pain that can be very hurtful to them. These children, who see their parents living in disagreement many times, wish that the bad would turn into good. And so, if they don't see it work out good, they may at times desire bad things for all good are lost for them.

Their minds can be damaged at school, unable to learn, not able to talk good to their friends and so on. They can find themselves following bad company. Then you'll be called on when in the hands of the police you'll see them. Or even worse going to the morgue to identify the body.

Will you allow your son and or daughter to tell you what you must do? Things may and are happening in families. But don't let it take root.

Marriage, instead of being the end of love, will or should be only the beginning. The husband and wife, mother and father, should show love by letting it rule the home. Let all practice self-denial, manifesting kindness, courtesy, and even from there one can learn sympathy. This love, true love will be kept warm in the heart, and he or she who goes out from such family to stand at a home of their own will know how to promote the happiness of the one which he or she has chosen for a companion for life.

A woman when having problem at home should never go to another man; telling another man what she's going through at home. This will not help but make things worse. He will show sympathy to you, but then you will have to adore him, even to worship him. Doing this, you are just putting more wood in the fire as some would say. He is going to offer you help, even to promise you that which he doesn't even have. Have you ever read that Satan the devil offered help to Yahshua after he was fasting for 40 days and 40 nights? Read that from *Luke 4, 1-14*; None of which Satan offered were not belonging to him so be careful.

The flour bags were used to make sleeping sheets for big people, also for babies. The bags were used for men and women underwear's, pillow cases, men sleeping clothes, diapers for babies, hand towels. Before using the bags, the women would wash them, put them to bleach, and then rinse them properly. Those women before would go to the river to wash their clothes They would select a special stone (rock). On this stone, she alone would wash her clothing. If any other woman were to use this stone, it would be after she's done using it. If she came back at any time and saw someone else using the stone she was using before she finished, she would ask this person to give up the stone. Each woman had their own stone.

Let me tell you another little something. When a young lady would bring forth a baby while at her parent's home, it was a shame to the family. The masquerades would compose many songs on this young lady. When the time to sing those songs on what we now call carnival day, the songs would go out openly on this young lady, not using her name, but they would use another name. If someone would let her know that the song was composed on her, she, if near, would seek to hide herself. Even so it was when husband and wife separated from each other. The behaviour of the many before was far better than what we have now. Not too many people feel a shame of their wrong doing it seems.

The government before was not allowing any kind of

song to be played in public. The songs were to be without any indecent languages. People are left to do whatever pleases them and for this cause the government get very little respect believe me.

Another advice to you my dear fathers and mothers. Take the cell phone from your child, read those messages that comes to your kids, let them know the reason for this strict rule is not of any hatred towards them, but when commanded; they must obey.

Remember your kids have no right to turn their backs on you when you are giving orders to them. Remember there are different levels of position in the family. Read what Paul says in *1 Corinthians 11, 1-3.*

This system of headship has been there from creation. Women should always be in subjection to the man in their life. Like it or not, that's what the bible says. **Genesis 3:16** says something very serious. Read what it says unto the woman.

Any woman who seems to disagree with these good teachings are attempting to overturn what Yahweh have already directed. When women obey these rules, there are sure blessings for her. Read what king Solomon said in the book of **Proverbs 13:24.** Also read **Proverbs 13:1**

Flour bags is what they were using to make what is known to us as pampers. At that time, it was known as diapers.

I'm going to tell you some things you know, and some things you don't know even of the old lifestyle. Many women would ask the shopkeeper to save for them some empty flour bags. That means after the shopkeeper finished selling the flour, the bag or bags would be sold to the women.

Pride has taken hold on us so much that we put away all those things that would help us have a life of less expense. Even so before, families that could not afford to buy bread, although bread was inexpensive, would roast one breadfruit or more, prepare it with some bush tea or cocoa tea and would have some cucumbers with roast salt fish as well with it. Nothing else did not taste as good as that.

Today we have all kinds of cream for use. Cream for babies, for men, for women, we have also oil for babies. But in early years, cream and oil for babies were not common. The most common oil and cream one could get was the Johnson baby oil and cream, also Johnson's baby powder. Castor oil were used to comb baby's hair, even to cream babies.

What About Light?

COCONUT OIL, KEROSENE OIL, CANDLES. These were used for lights by many people. To use the coconut oil for light, we would get a glass, put coconut oil with water, adding more oil than water because water is heavier that oil. Then place a mesh in the oil. We would then tie a very small piece of cotton in the middle of the mesh floating above the water and oil. When that was done, one would light it. When the oil consumed, the light would get into the water and that would shut down the light. Then more oil would be added in the glass to get the light back on again.

Now we are surrounded with lights. We have made ourselves so accustomed that when there is no light, the people complain more and faster than those who were raised without light in their dwellings.

Candle

USING CANDLE CAN BE VERY dangerous especially at nights. We had to be very careful when placing the candle. The kerosene oil I remembered seeing my mother putting kerosene oil in a bottle. Then she placed a little cotton or a little piece of cloth on top of the bottle, cut the cloth thin and long enough to meet the bottom of the bottle. The top of the cloth must be bigger to hold the light burning.

After she lit the bottle, she placed the bottle on a table, held a cup with water over the lit bottle, held it until the water got hot and boiling ready to make coffee. This I remember up to today.

Before and After School

IN MY SCHOOL DAYS BEFORE leaving for school, many of us at that time had to do our home chores. It would be carrying water, going to the pasture, sweeping the yard or house, washing dishes, etc. After school, we went to get water, scrubbed the floor, learned how to wash, went back again to the pasture to tend whatever animal we had. I learned to do all. At that time men were the key support for their home. Sometimes he brought in what he found, other times he would find nothing to bring. Still those women would understand them.

After world war two, things were very bad. Times were hard. Our parents could not afford to buy for us pretty pants and shirts for us. Most of our clothing were made with kaki and brown dungarees. That was very common. Many parents could only afford to buy the khaki. It was not so rough to wear like the dungaree. Some types of khaki were looking very good and shiny. Then after that came the polyester. Still, not anybody could afford to buy it.

Once upon a time my mother sent me to bring her

some sea water. When I brought her the sea water, she put it to boil. Then it turned into salt and that salt was used for cooking and for other uses. I'm telling you the truth.

At that time there were no Nido milk and all the different milk that we have now. But arrowroots were used to feed babies, along with the mother's milk that came from her breast-feeding. The adults and others were using bush tea or cocoa tea. When there was no meat, most women would find a way to cook. Some of them would use a coconut with some dasheen bush. The younger children used to grind the coconut, use the juice to mix with the dasheen leaf and with other things they got. When cooked, men I tell you, you should be there to eat from that you could have well bite your fingers.

Today with the many things to eat, it's not so. Most of our ladies would not cook since he brings in no meat. Please don't get me wrong. According to what I'm hearing, some would say; "what am I doing with a man that cannot put meat in my refrigerator? Who cannot give me shopping money?"

Not too many of these women could afford what they really needed. They would not put pressure on their husband for things they needed. Children when having just one pair of shoes, they were very glad. They had to know where they were placing their foot, watching their steps that they don't damage this precious thing, because if they destroyed the one they had, it was hard for them to get another one.

For a cap, for a pair of shoes, for pants or shirt, for food or drinks or anything given to them, they were thought not to forget to say thank you. Sometimes, they were saying it over and over again with a nice face. But the big problem is that when anything was given to a child, the mother or the father also the person who gave such thing to the child, were expecting for the child to say thank you. Should they fail to say thank you, the person giving something to the child would hold it back until they get to that point.

Today's time, there are some of them that have more than they can handle but the respect is not with them at home. Not even on the streets. Some children don't want to say thank you to anyone after receiving what is given to them.

Scrubbing the Floor

To scrub the floor, most of the parents would send us to bring some bay sand, some breadfruit leaves, soap and water. Sometimes, we the children would use the hard coconut shell with the bay sand and soap. But when that scrubbing was done, the flooring was clean. It stayed shining for weeks.

Presently we have so many things to do the job. But how many children although we have all these things to do the scrubbing are willing to do it when they are asked to do it?

At the time that I was raised, most men built their own home chairs to sit on. Chairs were not common as it is now. These pretty sofas we were not seeing very often. Probably in some places. We used to sit on the floor, and sometimes the father and mother would sit on the floor also especially when someone would come to see us. Don't think it's strange to hear. I just want you to say that you should be there to see that.

Let me say something to you reader. If you don't know

what I'm talking about, think. But be glad for the privilege of hearing, and seeing the many different things that are in the world. Say HalleluYah to Yahweh.

Maybe you know what a bench is and what its used for. It was very easy to build. I remember building two or three benches to sit on at home. My family was part of those that could not afford. On those benches, many times I would fall asleep.

Another one was the sofa. This was easy to build, it was made to sleep on. But many times, we were sitting on it.

Bread in The House

THERE WERE TIMES WHEN WE had no bread to eat before going to school. Some women like my mother, would cook food for us to eat before we left for school, or she would roast dasheen under hot sand. We would eat it for breakfast with a cup of cocoa tea. After which she would tell us to go to school.

Those blessed ladies were very helpful at home not tiring themselves in nothing when it was about home duties. They did it with love for their family. They never fell away from their duties. Thank Yahweh for them.

Today or presently our homes are jam-packed with all kinds of things that we hardly can move around. Yes. I know what I'm talking about.

One of the thing which people adopt is called "make-up." So many people using this thing. Even men find it good for them. There are all types of make-up.

People who put chemicals on their body and feel that they can do whatever pleases them for their body belongs to them, and that no one can tell them what to do, no one can stop them, listen to me. Take a good look at a baby. See if there is any such thing that the baby brought with him or her when they were born. I have seen so many people, young and old, and as I said, even men, when they are dressed and wearing these things, don't know how to walk. To them, others who are not wearing make-up are nothing. But can anybody give their make-up self to Yahweh as a sacrifice? Does Yahweh have a place in His kingdom for such people? I hardly believe that. All worldly styles will stay right here on this earth.

In The Home

THERE'S NOT ONE HOME WHERE the people don't get a little cut eye from each other, but when it is made known; my advice to that is you better try quickly to get it fix. Communicate with each other with love. Don't let the sun go down on your wrath says the bible, even if it seems impossible, no hope of fixing it. Many have left their home families and gone, with no hope of returning. It's not right for a man to runaway leaving the rest of his families behind. I call him a coward man.

But is it right for a woman to go away from her home family? I leave you to think on what I'm saying. 1 Corinthians 7: 9-11. Please don't be like the Prodigal son who went away from his father. Luke 15: 11-16 but are like him from Luke 15: 17-21.

The man and the woman that leave their home to have outside pleasure forget one thing but should remember first thing. Those children. Because while they are getting on with folly, their children or child are let loose on the street. So, say to yourself. I had my share, i enjoyed myself but my children are on the street. I'm returning home to meet them and getting them off the streets. Then you become a good prodigal father or a wise prodigal mother because I hated them at first and did love myself best. But now I love them more and it's good that I, now, hate myself. Read what happen to the prodigal son as he returned home to his father. Luke 15: 22-24.

It's my duty to tell you that this world with all its riches is not a haven of rest. There is a better place somewhere. For anyone to get there, we must hate this one with all its pleasure, live differently, serve Yahweh, be obedient all his Laws.

The Last Days

THE WORD OF YAHWEH SAYS that Those who will not agree to serve him are:

Self-lovers

o   Lovers of money
o   Boastful
o   Haughty
o   Disobedient to parents
o   Untruthful
o   Unholy
o   Without natural affection
o   Implacable
o   Slanderers

Without self-control

o   Fierce
o   No lovers of good
o   Traitors

o   Headstrong
o   Puffed up
o   Lovers of pleasure rather than lovers of Yahweh

Some Hold a form of righteousness but have denied the power of it. From these people, turn away.

Facilities

IN MY CHILDHOOD WE HAD facilities but not as there is today. There are lights all over, computers, internet, button this and button that to press to make life more comfortable. Telephones of all types, communication is much easier, cable TV, videos of different kinds, clocks, electrics of all types, automobiles, airplanes without number, boats also without number, submarines etc.

I remember those who posted letters to other islands. Letters that would take days, weeks before it reached the destination. There were not many engines as yet. So, boats at that time were using ore or sails, also, more importantly by strength of wind, even still many boats still carry ore with them when going to sea.

Sometimes, when there would be no wind, they would have to wait until they got some wind again. Presently, some people have life so sweet that they care about no one else. They give no glory to Elohim.

From school before, when we arrived home after greeting those we met, we removed our school clothes, ate whatever we had if there was anything to eat. If they left for us a piece of cane or a piece of coconut, we would go under the mango tree to find some mangoes. After we had a snack, there's no time or just little time left to play. These fathers and mothers did not like us to be idle. When my neighbouring friends came home to play when they were given a little time, my mother would say to us before we played that we must clean the basket of coffee. In that basket of coffee were little worms, and they were climbing on our hands. We were not at all pleased but could not say anything, we just did what we were asked to do.

The reason for leaving the coffee to rotten is because it cleans better and faster. The only problem was the worms that were climbing on our hands. To be honest, I did not like it. But liked it or not, we had to do it. After the cleaning we had a little time to play. As quickly as my mother noticed it began to get dark, she would ask all my friends to find their homes although we were not staying too far from each other. Those neighbours and my mother had the same rules of raising or training their children. They were agreeing so good that when they cooked, they would send from what they cooked for my mother, even so, my mother to them. How loving that lifestyle was before!

I wonder how many fathers and mothers care about their children, what they do, where they go, who they follow, what do they eat, how do they dress, etc. In the time that I was raised, my siblings could not be on the streets at night. It could happen only if an adult was with them. If they had lessons from school, that was done mostly at night. And at that time, lights were not common. Doing their lessons, they would go so close to the lamp to be able to see. At times they were having their heads so close to the lamp, their hair would catch fire because the oil in the lamp was kerosene. Anyway, that way of life is past and gone. Praises to Yahweh the Almighty Father.

Shame enough that there are some children who don't want to study, nor will their parents see to it that they study. Fathers and mothers tell me. Do you prefer to see your children sitting in front of the television than to encourage them to take their time to study? Don't let your children be idle because time is precious. Remember Esau's story and how he sold his birth right. Show them to make good use of their time. Let them know that chances lost can never be regained. Believe me, not everything that comes from the television is good for the eyes.

Problem between neighbours

I ROSE UP AND MET neighbours having problems with each other. Just as it is now. No one would insult the other. They would only discuss on what caused the disagreement between them.

I have spoken about my mother and not my father. Yes, that's true. Why? Because I don't know my father, he died while my mother was expecting me. So, I was not raised up with my father. But thanks to my mother who went through all her poverty but yet she raised up her children. In those days, poverty was no shame, because mostly everybody was the same.

Do you know that in time past that the bridegroom was required to pay before marriage engagement, a bill of money or its value in anything, or other property according to his circumstances to the father and his bride to be? This was looked on to be a safe guard to the marriage relation, because a father did not at that time think it safe to give the happiness of their daughter to any man that had no means to support his family. He should at least have a land, business, cattle or anything else. But a way was made to know those who had nothing to pay for a wife, they were permitted to labour for the father whose daughter they loved. When the man proved himself faithful in his service and in other services proved in true respect, the daughter would be given to him to be his loving wife. So, the payment which the father had received on behalf of his daughter was given to her at her marriage. If It was possible, I would still carry out this rule today believe me. When one fell in love and even got married, there must be rules to apply and to carry out if the marriage should last. They must have an active and sound mind. The two must try to build a good principle. Character activates principles. The two, the man and the woman must get the heavenly character, the unity of love. Real love must be there. Don't leave behind the fundamental love. The truth must be abiding within both. The two must get the very same spirit. One self will not make it but the two.

In many homes where love is not found, a weak nerve takes place. We can know it in this way when the father, who is the king in the family, is putting his laws. There must be laws to guide the family. The mother at times may disagrees. She places an X, meaning she prevents or objects the father from doing what he thinks is best for his home family.

I think that it is the best for the mother who is the queen in the home family, when good rules are placed by the husband. support it and let the children obey. That way, when the mother passes her rule, the father, since it is good laws, should not prevent her from placing her good rules.

Don't put an X neither and say you are the man. Action like these can cause the family to break apart. So, let love be the key.

When I was going to school, the teachers or teacher would stand in front of the classroom properly dressed. For they were setting the example for us. Showing us, the children, how we should dress when coming to school. The teachers knew how to behave. Not only in the attire, but also to have respect for the children whom they teach.

When I went to school, these teachers would not stand before the class using indecent languages. They had respect for and towards the children. I cannot recall seeing any teacher falling in love with any school child. Whether it's a boy or a girl. In the time we are living now, some female teachers as well as male teachers, are falling into a love relationship with the students.

In those days, beating a child in school was alright with the parents. If things had gotten out of hand, parents would go to the teacher to have it fixed.

In the morning when the school bell rang, the children had to stand in line. At which time one or two teachers would come to see if we had comb our hair, finger nails should be clean, shirt must be inside the pant. We had to be sure that our teeth were clean. There were times when the teachers would use a weep to get us in line. They were using the point of the weep through our hair, if the point could not pass through, it means to them that we did not comb our hair. So that same weep they would use it on anyone whose hair was not combed.

School started at nine o'clock sharp. Reaching late for

school, we would have to give a good reason or else we would get a beating. We would have Morning Prayer before we sat in class, before we went out for lunch, and also back from lunch at one o'clock. Prayer before meals was called "Grace before meals." Prayer after meals were called "Grace after meals." And at three o'clock, we prayed before we were dismissed to go home.

There were no lessons in school called the sex lessons. Furthermore, we did not even know or hear about condom or any such thing. Much less to be given to us. Sex is so common now and condoms are all over the place. You can find some in your children school bag. Hence the result doesn't believe in what is called safe sex. Why should a child carry or use a condom? From the age of ten to eighteen years old, that child be it boy or girl, should never be in such custom. Proverbs 22:15, verse 6 also Psalms 127:1-5.

To me there's nothing, absolutely nothing called safe sex. But if I were to advice someone on sex, I would tell them not to have sex at all until after marriage. But concerning sex. Do you know that sex was given only to those that are married? Anyway, I suppose that you did not send your child to school to learn no kind of sex lesson at all. Refuse that kind of sex lesson from them before it gets too far. A child left to self can bring sorrow. No child has the right to decide. But for them to love their parents. For them to love their father and their mother they must be taught. What kinds of respect do you as parents expect from your children if you don't show them what respect is?

It's a very ugly picture when parents adopt their children

old habits. I say that because many times I see mothers and fathers doing things that are not good. Comparing them with the life style and evil doing that comes from their children. You should be to them that kind of shining light. Let them see all that you are doing is good. Fathers, you should not carry your child to the bar when you know that you going to have a couple of drinks.

It is not right for a man to fight his wife, or no woman at all, man, as well as woman, ought to give respect to the person they love. Husbands and wives should not Quarrel with each other, especially when the children are around.

Read what Elohim declared by the prophet in **Isaiah 5:20-24**.

Elohim has not put in his words no command that man may disobey and not suffer for it. If man choose any other way than that of obedience, mankind will find that when the command of Yahweh is disobeyed, men will pay the price of death. Proverbs 14:12. Do not learn the worldly ways. Are the worldly ways better than the ways of Yahweh? Of course not! When I was a young man, I never heard man marrying man, and woman marrying woman. In this age there is nothing wrong if a man wants to marry another man. Also, I never heard about any woman preacher. Now in these days, there seems to be nothing wrong for a woman to stand on a pulpit to preach even if she cut off all her hair on her head. For some, it is still something good she is doing. That same woman preacher can wear any short dress. Just let her preach what she wants and let the people say "Amen".

Read these bible verses to get a better understanding. Acts 3:19. 1 Timothy 2:8-13, I Corinthians 14:33-36. Today's time some people are living carelessly. It is because these people don't want to have Elohim in their lives.

Looking at A Wedding

WHEN I LOOK AT A wedding, I can always see people dress in blue, white, yellow, orange, green, black and so on. Men and women, even children enjoying themselves. Sometimes lots of vehicles, also with different colours. The people are eating, drinking, dancing, laughing and having fun.

After the wedding is over, everyone departs. Leaving only the man and the woman by themselves to work out their married life. If the man and the woman do good in the relationship, that's good., If not, it's sad for them. Ephesians 5:22-23, please read it carefully. From the nineteen forties, things have changed a great deal. In past years there were not many women going away from their husband doing as I told you before. That would look like a disgrace upon the family. Another little secret. The old people before who had money, gave it to no one to hold. They would hide the money not telling anyone where they hid the money. But where do you think they hide the money? Not far. They would hide the money in the house. In the mattress. They would tear a little hole in the mattress, and then push the money inside. Sometimes, if the person fell sick and died, no one knew that the money was hidden in the mattress. Sometimes, because of old age, they forgot where they put the money. So, these people loved ones never got to know where that money was. The people's custom was after the death of anyone, many of what that person were using must be thrown away. Including the mattress. So, a lot of money were thrown away.

Police and Priest

IN MY YOUNGER DAYS, PEOPLE had great respect for the police officer and for priest. Most of us were looking at a priest to be so holy that we did not want to have nothing to do with him. Some people, especially children, whenever we would see a priest or a police officer, we would hide ourselves. There were no female police officers in those days. People at that time were bowing to the priest. We were taught to walk very humbly before them. However, it's not the same now, the priest is not getting that kind of honour anymore, nor does the police officer. It seems that respect is nowhere to be found. Even the priest and the police have less respect.

It was said before that the men were the bread winners and that the women were to stay home to take care of the children and the home, while the man was out in the field. Now things have changed. Both men and women are out there. So now we have women pilots, women drivers, women builders, women painters, police women, female doctors and the list goes on.

Sometimes the women pay checks are higher than the men. Ah! Because of that some woman get loose. The man in the home has no value anymore. He is no worthier to be respected. Let us not forget that some are even going to the pulpit to preach while men are sitting and listening to them. I never thought I would live to see such things.

He who called the patriarch, judged him worthy. It is Elohim that speaks, he who understands the thoughts afar off and place the right upon men say, 'I know him.' There should be on the part of Abraham no betraying of the truth. He will not waver for selfish purposes as you find today.

He who keep the law and lead justly and righteously, would not only fear Yahweh himself, but would cultivate religion in his home. He would instruct his family in righteousness; the law of Yahweh would be the rule in his house hold. Abraham was loved by Yahweh.

Abraham, A Teacher!

ABRAHAM HAD IN HIS HOME a school and that school had over a thousand souls. Those who were led by his teaching, to worship Yahweh, found a home in his enchantment and there in that school they received such teaching that would prepare them to be the representative of the true faith. Thus, a great charge rested upon him. He was training heads of families, and his way of government would be carried out in the household even where they resided.

In time passed, the father was the ruler and priest of his own family. He had the right to exercise authority over his children even after they had their own family. No one was too big for the father to rule. Abraham's descendants were taught to look up to him as their head in both religious and other matters. Abraham wanted to present a system of government that would preserve the knowledge of Elohim. Genesis 18:16-19.

It was a great value for Abraham to bind the members of his household in other to build up a barrier against the idolatry that had become to widespread. Abraham, himself, seek in every way possible to guard the people of his dwelling against uniting with the heathen and witnessing their idolatrous practices. He knew that to associate with evil would corrupt the good principles that Yahweh taught them.

He took the greatest care to shut out all kinds of false religion and to empress the minds with the honour and glory of the living. Elohim has the true object of worship. Elohim, himself, had made the wise arrangement to separate his people as far as possible from connecting with the heathen. He made them a people that dwell alone, and not living with the other nations. It was Elohim, himself, who called out Abraham from those set of people that he might train and teach his family apart from the bad influence which surrounded them in a place called "Mesopotamian" and that true faith might not lose its purity through the descendants, from one people to another.

The love that the patriarch had for his house hold lead him to guard their religious faith; to give them a knowledge of what Yahweh wanted from them. They were all taught that they were under the rule of Elohim. Their children and they were to be no disobedience on the part of the children. Yahweh's law was given to each and only in obedience to it could people assure their happiness. In Abraham household there was not one law for the master and another law for servants. There was not a way for the rich and another way for the poor, no such rules were found. All both rich and poor were treated with justice and mercy. He will command his house hold saith Yahweh. He would not support the evil conduct of his children. How few are there today that follow that good example? On the part of the many parents there is blindness, parents neglected the love that they should prescribe to their children, and leaving them on their own way and having no form of discipline. When parents will not take a stand to command or to place rules on their children, leaving them in darkness it's a form of weakness to the children. According to parent's behaviour; many times, causes disorder. Children grow up with a heart not willing to do the will of Yahweh and for this cause the weak spirit in parents is transmitted to their children and not that only, but to their children's children. Take the example from Abraham and do to your household the very same. Let your rules be enforced as the first step in obedience, not forgetting Yahweh's authority. Remember that Yahweh means the Almighty, the eternal one, the powerful one, he is the creator, Yahshua is his son's name, who died to set the world free from sin.

Religious parents failing to walk in Yahweh's way, who do not keep the statutes of Yahweh, not obeying Yahweh's law, their youths as they make homes of their own feels no obligation to teach their children what they themselves have never been taught and you better believe that. For this real reason so many homes run without having Yahweh in them. Not until parents themselves walk in the law of Yahweh with great fear and a perfect heart, will they be prepared to teach their children after them.

Some parents need to be reform. In like manner some ministers. They need Elohim in their life and in their household. If they need to have a change, they must take his words to their families and let the words be their teacher. They must let kids know that it is Yahweh who speaks to them and these very words must be immediately obeyed. Never forget that our children must be taught kindly with love. Teach them how to live to please the great Elohim. The Bible should be the guide of their life and the coming tide of the evil world will not sweep them away.

It looks to me that in many homes, prayer is not taught. Parents neglect their duties to teach their children morning and evening devotion. They are not willing to take an hour of their time to give Elohim thanks for his great mercies, for sunshine, for showers of blessings, and for the rain that causes the earth to flourish, and for having the holy angels to guard us.

The abiding presence of Yahweh has found no place in their lives. In the homes we must seek Yahweh's guidance. What name should we give to these people who go through their daily routines not thinking about the great Elohim of heaven? They live their lives so precious that that permits them to be hopelessly lost. Yahweh said I know him. Him, meaning Abraham that he will command his household after him. How many home leaders can Yahweh say that?

Fathers and mothers, can you say in your house there rises another Abraham, another little Joseph, another little Samuel, another Esther, or another little Ruth, another little Moses, another little Isaac, and above all another little Yahshua?

Back to marriage. I look at a wedding ceremony so closely that I see one thing in resemblance. And that is a service given to a dead person. When someone is dead, you'll find most of the time that there are people who comes to assist. Some will stay around until the dead makes its way to the burial grounds. At that time, we'll see people having different colour of clothing, all type of vehicles.

While the dead lies at home still, awaiting to depart to its burial place, the people are giving jokes, they are singing, some are crying. In some countries, they play dominoes. Just after the dead make the grave its home, all jokes and crying are done. The dead is placed in its tomb, never to be seen again. The dirt is spread over the tomb, people are leaving for their homes, leaving only the dead person in its home. Even those that are in charge will leave it there; never to meet or see again. I look at that similar to a person who is getting married. But the difference is simple. With the marriage, life continues. Good or bad it's their business. If they make it good, good for them. But if they make it bad, too bad for them. When the wedding ceremony is over, all those that were there will leave only the two. The husband and the wife will carry out their life. So, life continues with them but with the dead, life ends.

In my early years when someone died, loved ones would come to assist. Some would do the laundry, scrubbed the house, swept the yard and cooked for everyone to eat. The carpenters would come to help in building the coffin. At that time, the name "casket" was unknown. The carpenters would have the coffin built on the spot.

One did not even need to have thousands of dollars to bury the dead. Today, what is the cheapest casket in price, do you know? While the coffin is preparing the dead person is still in its home. Not as we have it today. They did not know about putting the dead person in ice to preserve it longer. But when the time came to take it to its death place, that's the longer it would stay.

Before leaving to go bury the dead person, a person who could blow a shell would blow that shell once, twice, three times. The first blast and the second blast were to make people know that the dead is about to depart from its home. But the last blow is longer, and means that the dead is leaving to its home in the grave. When blowing the shell, there must be time between each blast.

To carry the dead in the coffin, four men would come to shoulder lift the coffin. If long distance, four other men would take over from the first four men until they reach to the burial place. What was good is that everything was done free of charge. Today everything is for money not free anymore.

Some people when having a dead to bury are very worried because they have no money to bury the dead. But the dead must be buried. The cost of burial is not free as it was before. Price ranges from as low as thousands of dollars and that is where the big headache is. Not being able to get that sum of money. The system is bad. Now the big question after all that expense for a dead person is, what good will that do for the dead person? Let's leave this system behind and think about those who are unable to start with the thousands of dollars to bury their dead. What must they do? For the time is getting harder, people are dying, and the dead must be buried.

Don't turn me off because I am telling you the truth

in all that is written here. There are some people who will try to follow the system anyway. Although they don't have that amount of money to buy a casket, they will go through all lengths to get that kind of money to buy the prettiest casket to please others. More like a show off. One need not to bury in a fancy casket. If you can afford it then that's fine. Without a pretty casket the dead will bury. It's not in what you bury your dead person that counts or how the dead is buried. Most importantly is the kind of life the person lived.

King Solomon was the greatest king that ever lived, read what he said in Ecclesiastes 12: 7-8 "Also in Ecclesiastes 9:4-6.

When I grew up and began to gain knowledge, the people at that time made great use of the moonlights. We used to play lots of games. We had camp fire nights, and that was very good moments. We used to sit with each other giving stories. Each person would try to give a story better than the one before. We boiled breadnuts at moonlight times.

In places where there were no lights, the people used to be very happy to welcome the beautiful moonlight. Tell me what became of the moonlight now? Who is making use of it? We are still having beautiful moonlights but not too many people are making good use of it as we use to do before.

Fighting with each other. People used to fight before as well. But one would hardly find a weapon from those who were doing the fighting. They would fight each other yes. But as soon as the fight ended, the fighters would shake each other's hand and go have a drink together. They would be hugging and kissing each other like they never fought. Compare that life back then with the now life. Presently there is not that kind of life.

Often, I hear people talking about having a good time. So, I'm asking myself what good time are they talking about? To many, having a good time is to go shopping for all kinds of things to put in their homes. Good times for them is going dancing, going to the beach, driving out with other friends, having many shoes, clothing and hats, a pretty house and more.

None of the above are not giving one a good life even if one may think so. All of these don't make a man complete, Ecclesiastes 12:9-14. Sir, lady, you might as well have all of the things you need, it's true. But what about your little ones? Are they at home when you need them? What are they doing outside in the dark at nights? Many times, you who have all these things in common can't rule your child or children. These are they you'll find roaming the streets, sons and daughters smoking, using illegal substances etc. These are the ones you'll find many times if married, not with their mate. And these are the ones you may find many times standing before the judge for evil doing. It's very easy for you to find them lying on hospital beds. Ecclesiastes 12:13-14.

If you obey and do what is taught, you are sure to receive a blessing. That blessing will give you everlasting life. There are so many people who feel that to greet somebody else will take away their value from them. There are others, who live on this earth and to them, there are no one else to fit in their shoes. Some of those who take the elevator see themselves in this way the big and small alike.

But if these people would just say a simple prayer, maybe, there would be a change in their life. A simple prayer as this: "Oh Yahweh, please have mercy on us, please teach us what is called good time or good life, HalleluYah".

Read Ecclesiastes 12:1-8

Now if you do not have a bible in hand, you must now get one because you must go on reading unto verse nine of the same chapter. Now let me say a little something to you which I believe you'll be pleased to hear. In many yards where people live, you can see one, two, three, sometime even four vehicles. Some are well taken care off. But what is also true is that just like these yards are having all these vehicles, so in many homes there are one, two, three even more bibles. Even in lots of offices we can find them. They call them The Holy Bible. The true question is; How do you handle and study your Bible? Do you open your Bible with care the same way you open your car door? Do you understand it, your Bible, the same way you drive and understand your vehicle? Do you treat your Bible the same way you take care of your vehicle; washing and polishing it?

Adultery

MY SON, PAY ATTENTION AND listen to my wisdom and insight, then you will know how to behave properly, and your words will show that you have knowledge. Listen now young men and all. The lips of another man's wife may be sweet as honey and her kisses as smooth as olive oil, but when it is all over, she leaves you with nothing but bitterness and pain.

She will take you down to the world of the dead. The road she walks is the road of death, she stays not on the road of life, but wonders off, and does not realize what's happening. Now listen everyone and never forget what I'm saying. Keep far away from such a woman. Don't even go near her door. If you do, others will gain the respect that you once had, and you'll die young at the hand of merciless men.

Strangers will take your own wealth and what you have so be careful that you don't find yourself sleeping or lying on your death bed; and that even what you have laboured for someone else will take. Hope that your flesh doesn't rotten away. It is better to listen now than to say later if you had gained wisdom and that you should have let someone give you correction. It might be too late to say give me correction that I may follow, and that i should have paid more attention to the preacher. And because you did not listen you now see yourself a public disgrace. Men must be true and faithful to their own wife, and only to her you should give your love. Men, you must be careful with children that are not from your wife for they might never give you your honour.

It is better to have your joy with the wife you have. Only her love can make you a happy man. Call her to embrace you and enjoy her sweetness. But why should man give his love to another woman? Do you prefer that which is in another man's package than what is in your own package? Now listen woman; all the advice given to men, they are for you also.

Yahshua sees everything one does. And wherever one goes, he is watching the sins of a wicked man. He sets a trap and he got trapped into it, himself. For there was no self-control, for his foolishness sent him to his long home: the grave. Ecclesiastes 12:1-8; read it as though you are talking to yourself. Ecclesiastes 11:9-10.

Parents

INSTEAD, FATHERS AND MOTHERS GIVE way to their children to make their home a dancing hall. A place for romancing where other children come to learn and to do what I call in my own given name "the romancing dance". I would therefore prefer and ask that they should make their homes a place where these so call young lovers could come and learn to pray and to read their bibles; and learn how they ought to take care of their families. Family home, a place where respect dwells. I have seen that the young ones think that all is ok with them, but I'm here to say "No", all is not ok at all because the hour of Yahweh's judgement is at hand and who is able to stand? They don't have time now to learn how to sew a torn garment, or to serve a stranger who comes to their home. I wonder if, off course, some parents are afraid of their children. They sometimes let the children have rules over the home. There are plenty of things a young man and a young woman can do at home before wasting their precious life. Time is not coming better but worse. The old pants and shirts you didn't want to wear, soon and very soon those who are alive and remain shall seek to find them. And those young ones who did not learn to sew will now have to learn because they will need those broken pants and shirts.

Believe me or not, the lifestyle today and before are not the same, mostly everything has changed. To clothe one was cheap. But it was not easy for the men before to clothe their families and that is one of the reason why the ladies especially had to sew the torn garments. Some of them had so many patches that the real pant or shirt could hardly be recognised. I very much believe that such time is again coming, and it is not too far. So, whenever the time returns as it were before, what is going to happen to those people who believe it was shameful for one to carry a patch clothes; the pants and the shirts that was torn up and sewed? Our young people are not learning and preparing to do what our old parents taught us to do before. For this cause, the time I expect to come will be very worrisome for them. At that time some parents will be blamed by their children for not teaching them to be ready for whatever tomorrow brings. I don't always blame the children. For it is always the duties of parents to get their kids to do what is good always and not to see them idling their precious moments. The children came and met things as they are. They believe that's how it's supposed to be because you father, and mothers never made time to explain to them about life. It is profitable for parents to teach their children everything. Don't neglect to teach them to fear Yahweh first, then you as parents, and then themselves. They must learn from you to stand behind their own responsibilities.

Don't allow your children to use their bodies to please the world; let them know that they are precious in the eyes of Yahweh.

We must raise our children not only for their own good, but for our good also, Yahweh expect us to raise them in the good way that Satan will get no power over them. Especially when they are dwelling under our roof. They should have no chance for doing what is not permitted.

Why should we as mothers and fathers lose our rights of ruler ship over our children? We must not slacken. We must not be afraid of them. We should not give in to them because we think that we love them and that we must let them lead the way and we behind them. No not at all. If we close our eyes on them, we might easily lose them. Some might end up in prison at an early age, some might lose their life at an early age, or be paralysed. All these and more can befall them just because we fail to do our part or duty when we had to do it. As I have earlier stated, the job of raising children is not for the fathers only, but also for the mothers. Join hands and hearts, if you want good for your children, but if one is willing and other doesn't, there will be no success; justice and love for them must be dwelling in the home. The place for them in the home is not always in front of the television watching that which is not good for them, put away the control, stop changing channels, don't help in spoiling their young minds for tomorrow you might cry for what you helped them to learn. Sir, please don't join with the devil to let him take control of you and your family. Mothers should always agree with the fathers when they are taking the right stand.

Fathers should not feel that they are always right and that mothers have nothing to say to them even when they are wrong. Women must always remember that they are the weaker ones and that the devil did not deceive the man Adam but the woman Eve; Genesis 3:1-24.

Satan has a very smart way to separate families from each other, placing the man one way and the woman another way. Also, the children. If women will occupy themselves more in the home, Satan will find very little or no chance to play in their lives. Know your values. Know your respect. Know that the home depends on you as the best piece of tool. Know your place and know Yahweh and love your family.

I wonder how many young people know that they have or had a grand old mother or a grand old father? I ask that because the way I see the young men and young women treat old people, they have no respect what so ever for the elderly. Too many young people, if they could crush the old, they would do it. But I thank Yahweh for taking great care and protecting the old ones. Praise Yahweh for his loving kindness. Some of the grand fathers and grand mothers are dead. But there remains some that if possible your kids should know them. Tell them their names. That is very important. Tell them where they are from. To those that are dead, let your children know the cause of their death.

Communicate with your children with love, although some parents need to know more things about life for themselves. Fathers should take the school to teach their boys before leaving the home to make a family of their own. How he should manage his own responsibilities. Likewise, you mothers must do the same to your daughters. Show them how to stand strong to shoulder good or bad responsibilities. If such schools are able to send out good students, we can believe for sure we will have less problems in family's relationship and the cry we are having today will be lesser in the community.

Question: Is a wife something that one can borrow or buy for any cause, or should they look for respect from their husband and others?

With what did children carry water before? I carried water in bowls and in goblets for a very long time before we could find something else to use. The boeri came from a boeri tree. Boeri can be used for many different purposes. The Boeri, when fully matured, people would split it in two halves. But before using them after splitting them, we had to have them well scraped and dried. We removed the seeds that were found inside. The seeds were very small or looked like the ones inside of a pumpkin. When these seeds are removed from the half, it should be well dried and scraped properly. Then our parents would use them as a dish because that is what we had along with other little things. Using it for carrying water we had to be very careful because it could be broken easily. Any mishandling while using them could get them broken. Many times, when going or coming from the spring as children, it could be that we were playing, or on a rainy day, the road would be very slippery. Causing us to fall. We were unable to save the Boeri from breaking when that happened. So how were we supposed to face our parents now that the Boeri broke.

Why was it such a big problem for us? Because we would be punished for breaking the Boeri. We had to be very careful.

There was also something called the steelpan. Men are using them even to this day. They removed what's inside and put it to dry. After which they bore two small holes in it. They put a little stick in each boeri. The stick should be in length nine inches. The stick must be inserted very tightly so that it cannot be removed by itself. After this was done, it would be used as a piece of musical instrument. There were little seeds placed inside of it as well. The person who used it must be able to follow well with the beat from other music instruments to have it all harmonized as one. Many times, we were sent for water before leaving for school, our distance to school was very far. We had no transportation to take us to and from school. Going to get water before and after school was not the only job we had to do. We also used goblets to put water because they kept the water cool and fresh to drink. The goblets were more fragile than the Boeri. Very easy to break. When handling a goblet, we as children had to be very careful that none broke in our hands. Today's time, I wonder how many homes have a goblet or where can it be found.

Everything is easier now. No more going for water, no more cleaning the rotten coffee. Nor do your children have to go to the garden or take care of the animals. Things have really changed. Family devotion is of most importance and should never be changed.

I remember seeing houses built but the flooring was bare ground. They did not have concrete floors which they would have to tile or carpet. keeping the floor clean was the children job. To keep it clean, the floor had to be swept daily. I believe if some of our children today, those on the streets running about, had someone giving them home chores, there would be less kids on the streets both night and day.The way some young women wasting their time now, it was not so before.

The key reason why children before were obedient was because the fathers and mothers were raising their children together. Love was prevailing more between them. They were "Seeing Eye to Eye". Too many divorce is going on now and that is causing a breakdown on our youths. Should you, husbands and wives forget, I'm privileged to make it known to you that the two of you are no longer two separate being, but one. One in unity, one in person having one mind, one love. A love that will create a partnership, a long partnership. Longing to be with each other all the time. Wishing to be with her / him always, when she is there, and when she is not there. In health and in sickness until death do you part.

You men should never stop buying the gift that you use to bring her when you wanted her love. It is good for you to still bring her gifts. When was the last time that you told her that you loved her while having a smile on your face? Now you became his wife, you forgot that you used to set the table and called him to eat when you were sitting together to eat? Why do big people forget their good habits? This is the man you must love and to him you must give your love. She is the woman you should love to have and to hold. Why should you forsake him for someone else, and why should you hate her for someone else? Remember the time when you went with her to buy the pretty dress, knowing that you'll be getting married to the most loving lady in the world? Remember also lady the time when you wanted him to buy that suit knowing that you'll be getting married to the most loving man in the world? There was joy in both of you, longing and hoping to see that day come when you will hold her and kiss her. Not forgetting that both of you vowed to each other for good or bad, for richer or poorer, in sickness and in health, till death do part.

Have it always in mind you husband and wives these vows that you made to each other and apply them if you want to have a happy relationship. When these vows are carried out, others will see, and the desire will take hold on them.

Adam was not supposed to hide in the garden, but to dress and keep it. Adam had to be a saviour to his wife, not a warrior, and his wife, Eve, had to be at her best with him in the beautiful garden. At that time, no temptation would befall her. Genesis 2:15-24 and Genesis 3:1-24.

A woman should be pure in heart than to have the outside of the body clean. Listen to what the apostle Peter has to say in 1 Peter 3:1-6.

Peter supports Paul's admonition where he indicates that women should not give a show with an outward appearance, he warns about how they should comb their hair, wearing of jewellery, and the way they should dress. By not doing such, the good attitude of the heart is lacking.

Peter and Paul said that the outward appearance is not important as the inward man. However, we realise that Yahweh declared that what is in a person's heart will emerge.

Mark 7:21-23. If some women will conduct themselves properly, they would remove some of the prejudice. They should carry a wise and quiet spirit. Peter goes on to say that those ancient believers like Sarah rely surely upon the beauty that comes from within. Sarah carried a very good spirit within her and that attitude is above any price. Sarah was submissive in her attitude towards Abraham. She showed him respect. She found her place besides him full of the heavenly grace. She agreed that Abraham was the head of the home. Men are supposed to take the example from Abraham. Likewise, the women from Sarah. Sarah had jewels in her home, but she did not give that value over Yahweh and over her husband Abraham. Those things we hold so precious apart from Yahweh, we must leave them out of our life.

From 1 Peter 3 verse 1 and onward, Sarah, the good and holy woman, got praised for her good character holding it to the point that brought example to all women. Peter felt obligated to that. In biblical times, those holy women who hoped in Yahweh used to adore themselves modestly and were very submissive to their own husband. Sarah knew that the best way to respect her husband was not by wearing jewellery or to dress in clothes where parts of her body would be showing as she made her way from her husband. This is one of these beautiful pictures that should hang on the wall; The Sarah picture. Sarah was using Yahweh and Yahshua's name in her prayers. These people never used another name at all.

Young ones. I did not have it as you have it. I was brought up having our kitchen outside in the open, in the back yard, Just the three stones that I talked about with no shade over it. Now listen. As I said before, this was nothing to be ashamed about. There were lots of kitchens like that. But now you have good kitchen. But, oh!! My people, you better close one eye and keep the other open for a time is coming and we don't know how it will be, but we may no longer have what we hold so dear.

It's surprising that from the kitchen to the house, sometimes the food would not meet those that were inside. It Would be that while my mother or my bigger sisters were preparing the food, it would rain, making the ground slippery. Eventually the one carrying the food for those that were inside, if not good enough to battle the slippery ground, would fall. Well if that person fell, the food is not good anymore. That's how it was in my early days.

I have reached a time when, so many different associations are giving their ideas about training children. Because of what these people are saying, most parents don't know what to say or how to act with their children anymore. Anyway, my question is; Where are these groups originated from? And who gave them the right to form groups and the right to prevent parents from raising their own children?

I'm presenting to you readers, some real people who have spoken to parents and even to children. The very first person is Yahweh himself who spoke to Adam and Eve, Genesis 1:27-28. The second is Moses from Exodus 20:12; and thirdly Paul in Colossians 3:20; read these verses more than once, Moses again in Deuteronomy 5:16 and Deuteronomy 6:4-9. With so many passages from the Bible to parents and children, how can these people give their own way for raising children? Are their ways better than Elohim's way? What is wrong with people? Where do they get their doctrine from? I think that the strength of parent in bringing up their youths is from the Bible. Paul calls the teaching going out from these people "Wiles of error".

Paul again in Ephesians 6:1-3. This chapter promises a blessing if followed, that it may be well with them and that they may live long on the earth. It is better if these people give way to fathers and mothers to nourish and nurture their children than for them to make rules of their own.

People listen. Please listen to me carefully and answer this question. When children live carelessly, and we are seeing many of them living a reckless life, what good do we expect from them when they are not following what those good and holy people said? Samuel has a question in first Samuel 15:22-23. Samuel was a prophet, read verse 24 of that same chapter. Saul agreed that he sinned. It would be profitable if there was even one group that would call those young ones and show them that it is wrong to disobey their parents.

Remember that Solomon was the wisest king that ever lived therefore his examples are set in:

- Proverbs 9:8-10
- Proverbs 12:1
- Proverbs 7:1-5
- Proverbs 6:20-23
- Proverbs 5:1-2

- Proverbs 28:13-25
- Proverbs 4:1-15

You can read the whole chapter. Also read Hebrews 12:5-15. There are many more good teachings for children in the Bible. But nowhere shows that parents should not correct their children. Leviticus 20:7-9; Exodus 21:15-17; Genesis 18:19. The father, the mother, the children, all must work together for their own glorious goods as a team. There must be no shaking heads, no pulling shoulders, and no division within the body. This body must always consider how soldiers are trained. It must carry along with it a strong unit. Each person, each one, the husband, the wife, the children performing his or her duty, assisting the family party to have its objective win, with the help of the Holy Spirit of Yahweh.

Let the older ones give respect to the young ones. The younger ones to the older ones must also give due respect for there must be respect in the body. Always have in mind that the man is the head of the body and let the woman be in subjection to her own husband says Paul in Ephesians 5:22-23. Likewise, you husbands must love and give love to your own wife and that will be the good picture to nail on the middle wall of each home.

In Today's time, we have what is called women's liberation movement. I wonder how many people are willing to look at these demonstrations. Perhaps you have seen such developments with the same sense as me while asking yourself the question. Where are all these movement and all these social ideas taking this world? Do you believe that the bitter fruits of social turn round can ever be reversed? Undoubtedly. And I also believe that this could be the reason why we have this high rate in divorcement. People take on their own doing what they want and what they think is best for them forgetting the facts that our heavenly Father is real and exists. If we seek the way of life from the almighty whose name is Yahweh, we will find that he has laid the best way which is his commandments. When an individual obeys its direction, it will produce happiness also joy and gladness, and that way will give us real guidance.

Perhaps I should point out that mankind has not very much success if floating around his own way. Especially now, mankind should return to following the scriptures for perfect change.

Families

WHAT HAS HAPPENED TO THE family unity in our lands over the past few years? Just as did ancient Rome, our nation or even nations are quickly losing the stability. Their strength that might be gain from a very tight family unit. When Rome became plagued with sin, divorce and illegitimate births became rampant. Today our world is falling away and following the same evil road.

I have proven, and you also have and are seeing that many men have and are losing their right as men that Elohim command to be the head over their family. He must stand for his right because he is the father, the husband, the priest. No one should try to take that away from him. After the past fifty years, man has taken a downfall and one better believe that. Other men or somebody else will want to tell him he has no such rights over his own household. So, he is standing under the west tide of life. He is standing under the bad rule of the mother and her children. But if the men of our country would take their powers and hold the authorities that Yahweh gave them, such misguided affaires as the women's liberation marches would never occur. More over if the father should take their rightful authorities; fewer divorce would this world have. With less of the juvenile and even emotional adding that with the bad influence upon the misguided children in our world today.

Sometimes the mother and the children never consider how hard the man work to sustain them. They see and know that the man leaves the house every morning to work. Could be six days per week, even seven days or even on his vacation. He leaves his home in the morning at six o'clock, seven days a week and returns at evening time tired from a hard day. Twelve hours out of twenty-four hours was dedicated to his labour but his family never sees this man. The man who leaves his home in search of bread for his family, they cannot say where their sustenance is coming from. Then some of them never realise how tired he is when he returns home.

In cases like these, the woman does not take the man into consideration. She might right away want something done by him in the yard. Such habits cause other incidents. Then problems mount to a high level in discussion. Finding more place will drift into the marriage relationship. However, since the man is the leader, the force directing his family, he holds this position. He must never think that he must rule his family with a hard face or in a cruel way like a tyrant, or ruling his family in terror. This man; the husband, the father, the very man in the house must discipline with love. He must not abuse ruling in such a way that it will accomplish a change in the children's and mother's behaviour. He must do all things to his family with the "Philadelphia Love".

Giving respect to the woman as the wicker vessel. Even though he is the master of his home. One of the strong passages regarding this in the entire Bible is found in Ephesians 5:22-23, read it with understanding.

Too many people take the relationship between a husband and a wife as a joke whereas it's not a joke at all. The wife should be in subjection to her own husband, as to Yahweh for the husband is the head of the wife, as the Messiah is the head also of the assembly, being himself the saviour of the body, says Paul.

The life of the wife should compare that which describes in 1 Peter 3:1-6. The wife should give respect to her husband in all her doings, even in her dressing, the woman who is reading this chapter ought to pattern her life from there on. These verses read, in like manner, you wives be in subjection to your own husbands that, even if, any obey not the word, they may without the word be gained by the behaviour of their wives. Beholding your chaste behaviour coupled with fear, whose adorning let it not be the outward adorning of braiding the hair and of wearing jewels of gold, or putting on apparel, but let it be the hidden man of the heart, in the incorruptible apparel of a meek and quiet spirit, which is in the sight of Yahweh of great price.

Now pay attention carefully as you read verses five and six, it says, for after this manner before time the holy women also, who hoped in Yahweh, adorned them, being in subjection to their own husbands. Now if you disagree with verse five then read verse six, but please agree. Which reads. Sarah obeyed Abraham, calling him master, whose children you now are if you do well. I like that part. It points out the seriousness of the whole matter if you do well and one not put in fear by any terror.

Now you thought since Peter was a man he had only what to say to women and not to men. But that was a grave mistake made by you men. Peter says. You husbands, in like manner dwell with your wives according to knowledge, giving her, her who? The wives you married, Honour. 1 Peter 3:7.

Liberated. Liberated from what? Certainly, I don't know from what the modern women wish to be liberated. In some of those countries, women have been accorded all best treatment. Except in certain cases of course, conveniences are available today.

When divorce occurs, the mother often forced to find ways to support her remaining family. Sometimes the children become wayward kids, left to go about with no one over them. They go along daily, idling their time and gets into trouble. On many Occasions, the juvenile courts must take over. By doing so, the government takes away those children from their parents.

Let me assure that it is not the responsibility of the government, the school or even your own religion to educate the child. In the bible we find passages such as Deuteronomy 6:6-7. The bible gives the responsibility to parents to teach their children the correct way of life and these words which I command you this day, shall be upon your heart and you shall teach them diligently to your children and shall talk of them when you sit in your house, when you lay down and when you rise up.

Juvenile delinquency

IF EACH PARENT WERE DOING what they are supposed to do, taking responsibility in raising their children or educating them, showing them what the commandment of Yahweh says, there would be less juvenile delinquencies and problems for you and the parents. Your children are commanded in the bible to love and to respect your elders. Read Leviticus 19:32. In this present age, the Bible and what it stands for is ignored. Isaiah the Prophet said a time will come. And this is what he said will happen. He said, and I will give children to their princes and babies shall rule over them. Read also Isaiah 3:4-5 and verses 12-13. And the people shall be oppressed, everyone by his neighbour. The child shall behave himself proudly against the old man, and the base against the honourable. When a man shall take hold of his brother in the house of his father, saying you have clothing you be our ruler, and let this ruin be under your hand.

Problems From Television And Internet

IT IS TRUE THAT TOO many children are wasting their precious moments in front of the television. I have to include the parents also. And because what we learn must bear fruits, the mind many times got lost and falls into violence, murdering, robbery, crimes, broken homes and dirty comedies will play its rule. Not having a mind of reasoning, no power is valid enough to change the life conduct of these people. Even their personalities will become defeated.

Now what about the chat rooms and websites that are featuring pornography? I believe that this bad life style in our country can be traced directly from the television and internet. This good and at the same time bad tool has and is causing many people to damage their good senses. Then immorality takes over while the younger ones will go seeking to find the gratification of their evil nature. Now again, since that is so, it is good that parents are having their children go to school with a computer, or even have it at home to supervise them. Because without you doing that, it can be dangerous and cause damage of life. Instead of wasting time in front of the television, computer, internet; help them to find something more constructive for their minds.

Some children before suffered corporal punishment to discipline them. In my home town where I was raised, the disobedient children were handed over to the police station. The police would tie the disobedient child on a bench and whip him many times (a very good beating). After the child leaves the police station, he would never want to go back there ever again. He would even advise his friends not to find themselves there. When the police untied that child, the body had big marks. Some of the marks blood appeared.

Now, such punishment is forbidden by law today. The children are left to do as they please and the whole world is getting worse and not better. But should action take place not allowing the youths to have their own way, getting them to change their evil behaviour, I think that the world would gain strength of character. I also believe that that old way should be implemented as a form of discipline. Anyway, that way of discipline has now become out and is illegal.

The children that I grew up with, were all taught to respect the rights of other people. If all the training ways of the old would return by any means, we would see a change from our young ones.

Many people have reached the point where they fill that they cannot, by themselves, withstand the drifting tide that sweep the world. If you are one of them, I am with you to tell you that you can determine to live in harmony with Yahweh's ways of life. Maybe you might be the only person in your neighbourhood. Nevertheless, your life may have upon those who live near you some positive influence so to change and a blessing will fall on you from the Almighty.

Everyone should realise that this world and its system is going to a dead end with no hope of returning. But the only sure hope is that Yahweh is calling a people from this dark world of sin. Proverbs 9:11-12. The time for our heavenly father to judge this sinful world is at hand. Now is the time for all changes to take place, now is the right time for one to start experiencing the joy of living for our heavenly father by placing your life under the direction or Yahweh's word.

The Key To Knowledge

THE FIRST KEY: READ ONLY the first part of Proverbs 30:28. The second key: Proverbs 30:11-12, let them know who to follow and who not to follow. The third key: Proverbs 29:15, let them know that the rod is good. But both the rod and the reproof walk together for they give wisdom, and does not say that the parents must not weep the kid. Only the system says we must not. Proverbs 19:18: This verse says that you should chastise them and don't feel soft hearted towards them because of their tears.

Proverbs 13:24 and Proverbs 8:32-35: These verses are talking about attention. Proverbs 6:20-22: These verses say to listen to fathers and not to forsake the law of mothers. Proverbs 7:1-4: These verses explain if the child wants to live long, what he or she needs to do. Deuteronomy 5:16, Exodus 20:12; Proverbs 5:1-2, Proverbs 4:1-6, Proverbs 3:1-4, Proverbs 2:1-2, Proverbs 1:8-19. Always remember that you were placed here for a purpose, and is to love and serve Yahweh. Let all children bring, give respect to Yahweh first, then to men and to self.

It appears that the average person doesn't know what true love is. True love is not when one carries you to the club or having a party life. It is not because one carries you in the bar. It is not found in the beer bottle, it's not there roasting on the grill. It is not to kill but to be killed. St Johns says in chapter 3 verse 16, that true love must come from within your own self, you. Romans 13:8-10: To those married ones I say remember your duties. Read also 1 Corinthians 7:1-12, 1 Corinthians 13:1-13.

Please read Jeremiah 25:30-34.

All these must befall men because Yahweh is no more pleased with the doings of men. Mankind has taken their own way doing only those things that pleases them. Read Psalms 59:1-8. As they reject Yahweh's rules of life and say there is no Yahweh. So, will Yahweh put in them an open shame? You better count on that.

The shepherds shall have no way to flee, nor the principles of the flock be able to escape the voice of the cry of the shepherds and the wailing of the principle of the flock; why? For Yahweh lays their pasture waste and the peaceable folds are brought to silence, why? Because of the fierce anger of Yahweh.

He has left his curvet, as the lion, for their last has become an astonishment. Why? Because of the fierceness of the oppressing sword, and because of his fierce anger, Jeremiah 25:30-38. You see, people must not think that Yahweh is a playmate that we can do to him what we want, and that we can serve him in our own way. We can go to service and dress as we want and act as we wish, thinking that it's ok with Yahweh. Yahweh doesn't like the way you dress showing your underarm. He doesn't like your hair style, nor your hair cut. He wants holiness from us. Not our style in which we serve him, but to serve him the way he asks us.

Remember Cain and Abel, Cain's offering was not accepted. Leave out your own way of serving Yahweh and give him the way he asks for. In this manner says Yahweh, stand in the way and see, and ask for the old paths, where is the good way and walk in it, and you shall find rest for your souls, but they said, we will not walk in it. And I set watchmen over you saying, listen to the sound of the trumpet, but they said we will not listen. Therefore, hear you nations, and know you congregation, what is among them. Hear o earth, behold, I will bring evil upon this people, even the fruit of their thoughts, why? Because they have not listened to my words and so for my law they have rejected it says the Almighty, Jeremiah 6: 16-17.

Today, in our time, there are preacher's men and women preaching a "No law" doctrine. Telling people that we are not under the law but under grace. I have these words for them. Grace is not a licence to do as you please, Yahweh will send a curse on this land because people will or don't want to be in an assembly that teaches them law keeping. They want to go to church because church going, and church building has become so common in our time that one can just build a church and put anybody to preach as long as money is coming in, and that is the reason why so many people goes there. They can come how they want to, who cares? They can do what they want to that's their business. So, Yahweh will judge this sinful world. How do you say we are wise and the law of Yahweh is with us? But behold, the false pen of the scribes has worked falsely. Yes, they leave out the name Yahweh and Yahshua which means salvation and inscribe the Baal which means The Lord. The wise men are put to shame; they are dismayed and taken. So, they rejected the name Yahweh and his words.

And what manner of wisdom is in them. Therefore, will I give their wives to others; and their fields to them that shall possess them everyone from the least even to the greatest is given to covetousness. In the eyes of many people nothing is wrong. They see nothing unclean, but all is clean. They can eat something even if Yahweh put unclean stamp on it, yet it is good for food. Even if Yahweh rejects the keeping of their feasts days, they will regard it as good. I never see more churches as I am seeing right now. It is like a game that anyone can play. Someone build a place, get a name for it, take anyone who shows interest gets in. Even if it is a woman behind the pulpit to say anything unwise with a little truth. They play the music loud that its members can dance. Then collection is made, two or three times or as much as possible as the doors are open for people to come in. I believe many people have seen that but who cares?

Jeremiah says, from the prophet even to the priest everyone deals falsely. Read Jeremiah 8:8-10. Also, Hosea 4.

With the understanding of what you read compare it with the now life. You who read must agree that the prophet was making no mistake when he wrote that. Really, our world is full of gross evil; evil of all kind.

There is nothing but swearing and breaking faith. Killing, stealing, committing adultery, they break out. Blood touches blood. The land shall mourn and every one that dwells in it shall languish, with the beast of the field and the birds of the heaven, yes, the fishes of the sea also, shall be taken away. Let no man quarrel, neither let any man reprove.

So many things are happening in our lands, yet the churches are preaching a "No Law" sermon but save under grace. And they believe that because they are under grace, they can go on doing away with the law of Yahweh, breaking truth is very easy. The man and the woman get married in the space of six months they can be seen standing before the judge, arguing with each other seeking for divorce; the bad trying to win the good. The prophet goes on to say, for your people are as they that quarrel with the priest and you shall stumble in the day, and the prophet also shall stumble with you in the night. And I, says Yahweh, will destroy your mother. Very strong and serious talk.

People listen, we haven't heard, nor have we seen anything as yet. In coming years, just before the Messiah returns; those that are not dead, having eyes and ears will see and hear what they never thought. Yes, now things are going well our way. Life is sweet, ok! But what are we going to do when these terrible times fall on us? To who will we call, and on whom will we depend for safety? Which name will you call?

My people are destroyed for lack of knowledge. Because you have rejected knowledge, I will also reject you. That you shall be no priest to me. Seeing that you have forgotten the law of Yahweh, I will also forget your children. As they were multiplied, so they sinned against me. I will change their glory into shame. They feed on the sin of my people, and set their heart on their iniquity. Hosea 4:1-8.

The Bible says that marriage is honourable, but how many people realize that? The dictionary definition of the term marriage if you have never learned that yourself, here is the definition in the Webster new world dictionary of the American language second college edition.

First, the state of being married, relation between husband and wife, married life, wedlock, matrimony; if you read the note from the synonym section appears the following: a man and a woman who have become husband and wife the state of relation between them in marriage or to the ceremony making this unite. Therefore, little doubt is possible. Think on the word Marriage. Claim it as a union. A place within a man and a woman, and together each one is committed as husband and wife. What other meaning has the religious sacrament of marriage? The religious sacrament has or had no other meaning but to bind together the two, one female with one male, one man and one woman under biblical law. The Bible does not in any way give rights for man and man to join themselves together in marriage, nor woman with woman. No such committed relation should exist between homosexuals and lesbians. Leviticus18:22 and Leviticus 20:13.

Almost every day we go to the supermarket to buy what we need. And so it is very easy for us to find raised prices every two weeks or so. Remember Revelation 6, The world is becoming worse and worse and that is a sure sign that the man of sin will soon take his seat and then comes wars, dangerous wars. Then the next step is the Messiah's return.

Parents never forget that in Deuteronomy 6:4-9 and in Deuteronomy 18:19, that Yahweh warns the people of Israel to be careful not to learn, not to do, not to follow the ways of those other nations. There are people who know Yahweh and will pray in the name of other mighty ones.

When a storm passes and damages houses, trees, such as bananas, coconuts, oranges, grapefruits and so on, the people will go to church for a little while, praying often to their mighty one or mighty ones. But after all is over, and life gets back to normal, no more praying.

Restaurants

WHEN LAST YOU WENT TO a restaurant to buy a meal? What did you ask for, can you remember? Today in restaurants, all unclean dishes have a high price. Did you notice that? Or are you saying that there is nothing unclean? If you say such, I ask you. Have you ever cast your eyes on a chapter or chapters in the Bible that calls swine unclean? If not let me help you Deuteronomy 14:1-21; Leviticus 11:1-4.

Acts 10:14. Read the whole chapter for a better understanding. From this chapter you will read that Peter said he has never eaten any unclean or common thing. All unclean fishes are to be rejected and not to be eaten as you just read. Stop spending your money on unclean dishes. There are clean meats for you. Yahweh would never leave us without giving us what is clean and good for food.

DRUGS;

YOUR YOUNG ONES, BOYS AND girls, even some older ones are cut in drugs. I have noticed even little school children are falling victim to drugs. Some parents are seeing their kids falling victim, damaging their young lives, making them look so old, yet fail to take a stand to reform their life back. Parents must find ways and means to help their children to become men and women for a better tomorrow. Whipping a child is not a crime neither is it a sin. It is a way of nurturing the child. Please when using the whip, be very careful not to harm the child. Do not use the rod when you are vexed or in a terrible rage. Tell the child why you gave him the whipping. Never beat the child without letting him know the reason.

I have been seeing lots of things which I never thought I would be seeing. One of them is a pregnant woman, I have seen lots of them even my own sister, carrying the unborn. These women while pregnant, tied their stomach so that it would not be exposed. They would put a large cloth over their stomach. They would be so careful not to eat anything, not watching anything, not sitting anywhere, etc. The father sometimes would touch the stomach making jokes with her. Most of the time they were feeling so embarrassed that the men were to help them to do the house work. You see there was love before and the lovers were more loving than they are today. Many changes have taken place. Before when a woman brought forth a baby, she would stay in for about thirty days. After those days, she would go for a sea. She would bathe on the beach where the waves would reach her. There she would wash herself.

When she was ready to deliver, the husband or someone close to her would call the midwife. The midwife did not have all the tools we have now to do the job. Of course, she would have a pair of scissors and some other things to give the woman a clean delivery; to cut the umbilical cord or tie it. Then clean-up the child. They would constantly check the woman and child to see if everything was ok. There was a special bush they used for tea after delivery. It was used to clean the blood.

After the midwife cut the umbilical cord, when the placenta was removed, someone close to her would bury it in a hole and then plant a valuable tree over it and the tree would be for that child. Most people planted a coconut tree. There are some who never received baptism.

Having a baby and leaving that baby in the care of a baby sitter was not the custom as today's time. There are so many who were never brought to an assembly. They grew up living a life and never attending any religion at all. The problem is when that person died, that person's family is unable to find a place of burial. That was how it was back then.

Jumping the fence

I REMEMBER KNOWING SOME YOUNG ladies who brought forth at least one child while at their parent's home. Yes, it happened. These parents would say, but don't let it happen again. They would say it with a deep meaning that you would understand. You see, many times I use the words "those parents" because most homes had the very same rules. Sometimes, the young lady would try to jump the fence thinking that her mother did not see her, trying to leave her child to go out. Oh no! She has a surprise. All she would hear from her mother was "To whom are you leaving your child? Go with your child, don't leave your child with me, carry your child wherever you are going." She had no other choice but would have to either come back to stay or carry her child with her. Sometimes, if she wanted to go to some special place in advance, she would ask her mother to take care of her child until she returns. The mother if agreed, would let her go. I know in those days there was more respect from them to their parents than now. Parents would not have to say the same thing over and over to their children.

They had different methods to nurture their children according to the thing a child would do. It could be that they would withdraw one meal from that child. It also happened to me. While on my knees I remember seeing my sisters eating while having tears in my eyes. One of my sisters kept looking at my mother, hoping she would turn away or go out so that she would give me some food from hers. The rest of the children felt bad seeing that they are eating and one, be it a brother or a sister, was not eating. In my case, my sister would seek to find a way so that I would get a little from hers. But in doing that, she had to be very careful not allowing my mother to see her. If caught, my mother would value her as a rude child, for so it was in those years.

If a child was sent out by the parents for something or to do something, he had a limited time. Some parents, especially the mother spat on the ground and demanded from the child that the spittle would not dry out before that child returned. The child would try their best to return before the spittle got dry. As I'm writing that, I'm asking myself: What's the matter with the fathers and mothers now? How do they raise their children now? What training they themselves had? How were they brought up from their parent's home? What made the big old change?

You sent your daughter to school. You love her and that is very good. But you should not stop there. There's a lot more to do for her. You should not be slack with her and think to yourself that you love her too much to instruct her.

Some of them can be very stubborn. Sometimes from school, she gets pregnant. The first time you said nothing much. In some places she can still go back to school. So, what did she do with the first certificate that she brought home. You claimed it while she goes looking for a second one. She gets pregnant again. She brings it home. What are you going to do now having two false certificates? People the ugliest part is this young lady never told her parents who is the father of the babies. They have no idea. Or sometimes they do. The first and second time all your daughter knows is that her mother will take care of the babies and of course, the mother do take care of them, allowing the girl to go out partying all night, coming home weary and tired, wasting her precious life for nothing and you as the mother is supporting her. She comes home after her night of partying and will fall asleep as soon as she arrives home. You as her mother, are left to continue taking care of your daughter's child or children.

Some time ago, a lady came to me and said; "I don't know what to do with that girl, meaning her daughter." Before she could go any further, I said well that's good for you, for you wanted it that way. You are to be blamed for that because you as a mother agreed for all what she was doing. So, she asked me why would I say that. I answered her and said, because she is under your roof. I got a bad look from her, but I didn't care.

There was a time when I was a teenager, my mother sent me to the supermarket to buy her some alcohol because someone came to visit. I bought less alcohol than the amount she told me to buy. What I did was I took from the money to buy some other little things, and then I added water to the amount of alcohol to make it look like the right amount. When I arrived home with the half bottle of alcohol, she tasted it and said it was very light. She asked me to take it back to the shopkeeper at the supermarket. Well you know there was trouble for me. How to give it back to the shopkeeper? Anyway, I had to bring it back. When I went back to the supermarket to explain myself to the shopkeeper, the shopkeeper disagreed with me because the alcohol that was sold to me was very strong. So, the shopkeeper did not accept the alcohol that I brought back. I had to go back to my mother and tell her the truth. Believe me if you were there, I don't think that you wanted to be in my place.

My mother gave me a hard beating that day. Never did I do something like that again. You see children always do thing such as this. Parents who knows that their children are doing bad things like what I did should never slacken but stand against it at once. That is why when I see children doing all the evil they are doing now, I question myself. Where are the fathers and mothers of these children to stop their children from the evil of the day?

When a chance was given to us as children to play with each other, we would go playing. However, after playing, each child would go to their home. If when at home, our parents would find us having anything that was not belonging to us, they would question the child. If the object that they questioned the child about is not their belonging, the parent would ask the child to return the stuff to the rightful owner. Talking about the children and how we lived back then to many parents is a sin, but they believe that allowing them to bring home what is not belonging to them is righteousness. Anything, you did not give your child or children, when they came home with it, you the parents should question them. Don't keep your eyes shot so tightly that you cannot see the evil doings that they did. Because one day you'll have to open your eyes, ears and mouth to defend them before the police, at which time you'll say you have not heard or seen anything that came in your yard or in your house. Stand up, stand up, play your part; let your kids know that they cannot do what they want if they live under your roof. Isaiah 5:18. There is going to come a time when some of your children will blame you, because you upheld them in the evil they did and did not teach them to do the right thing.

I'm going to tell you something that I heard when I was a young man. A young man did something bad and the police got involved, the young man was arrested and a complaint was made against him, While standing before the judge, he was asked to say something. The young man asked to speak to his mother. The mother came forward. He then asked his mother to come closer so that he may whisper something in her ears. She came to her son expecting to hear something good. The young man held his mother and bite out one of her ears with his teeth. He then said to her; "Had you corrected me when I did wrong that would not have happened to me." Too late is always too late if you allowed your youths to steal, ill-treat people, lying, meddling in other people business and other things which you know and will not put a stop to. They will one day pay the cost, but you will cry because you failed to do your parental job. I heard they used to say the evil that people do live after them, but now I say that the evil they do live with them.

I am getting married one would say to someone else, he or she would answer; "really, you are getting married? I am so happy for you!" Then that person to whom the invitation was given would bring what he or she could afford when going to the wedding party. That was the custom before not too many years ago. But now big changes have taken place.

Today, someone would say to his or her friend, "I'm getting married." That friend's response would be, "is that so? well I'm happy for you." Invitations goes out to whom they chose to invite to their wedding. Sometimes you'll see that the person that sent out the invitations, tells you what they would like you to bring as a gift, and they will tell you where to buy that which they are asking. Regardless, if you find it somewhere else or costing less than where they sent you, but you must buy it where they sent you because they priced it. They know the cost of what they are asking for. So, it is not you anymore giving the gift, but they are taking a gift from you that you may not be able to afford. But wanting to please them, you went out of the way. Now what do you say about the time in which we are living? Is it not demanding to follow the system?

I will go to no such wedding. Do not send me any invitation. I'm not going with the system because no one is marrying for me, nor am I marrying any one in that system. Some marriages are not what or how they used to be before. They don't carry any good meaning, and it has lost its honour. Some don't marry for the real reason as before. They are marrying the person for what he or she has and not because of love. It's like putting a sword in one's flesh. You must marry for no other reason but for love and love only. A Love that will grow daily from both the man and the woman. Not one that is weakening daily.

If before you get married you know that you don't really love him or her, you better don't do it. If you think that the only way to get what you want is to get married, then don't. If you don't have love towards your spouse, whatever you may possess because of the marriage, won't bring you love. Love must be there to fulfil the royal law.

The modern-day churches will have you to believe anything you do is ok with their heavenly father. Come as you are, you don't have to repent. One Sunday morning, I went to a place near a church. People were going in, I saw a lady going in with her dress having a long split open from her thighs all the way down to below her knees. That same lady had her hair braided and falling on her back, having no covering on her head. I heard them singing happy birthday to someone.

Soon after, I saw a young fellow going in while pulling up his falling pants. You know the style! You know what I'm talking about. Some have sleeveless tops showing their underarm. Some are having other hair styles thinking that is their style the heavenly father is interested in, no not one inch. I *Samuel 15:22-23*. Samuel says; Has Yahweh as great delight in burnt-offerings and sacrifices, as in obeying the voice of Yahweh? Behold, to obey is better than sacrifice and to listen better than the fat of rams for rebellion is as the sin of witchcraft and stubbornness is as idolatry and teraphim. Because you have rejected the word of Yahweh, he has also rejected you from being king. The serious point is this Yahweh has no favour for kings, princess, or anyone for that matter. All he wants from us is that we fear him and that we keep his commandments. *Ecclesiastes 12:12-14* not in your styles you carry. *Isaiah 58:1.*

Parents are you ready to do your training job? What will you give in exchange for the life of your children? Remember *Deuteronomy 6:4-9*. Some years ago, I went to an island on Yahweh's business. I Went on a passenger bus. I sat in the middle of the bus. On my right was a young lady with her little girl child about three or three and half years old. As a child she began playing with my beard, as the custom of many of them does even at home. I allowed her to play with my white beard, The child then tried to embrace me on the mouth with her tongue. when I saw what she is trying to do, I ask the mother who was a young lady if she saw what her daughter was trying to do. She said yes, I said to her you are to be blamed for that, because the child has seen someone do it. So, I ask her to stop doing that. The other passengers heard me telling the young mother that.

Many mothers especially, think that a child at this age don't know much so they will do what they please in front of the child. What I want to say is this; The children now are not as those of yesterday, so take no chance with them. From Isaiah 58, Yahweh ask or command Isaiah the prophet to cry aloud, spare none, hold back nothing from the people, lift your voice like a trumpet. Why should the prophet do that? To show the people, declare to the people their transgression, and to the house of Jacob their sins. Verse 2 says; Yet they seek me daily, and delight to know my ways as a nation that did righteousness, and forsake not the ordinance of their Elohim. You can go on to read the chapter, but when you read the thirteenth verse, pay special attention to what it says.

What punishment can you give to your child who doesn't obey the rules of your house? Can you as a parent see your child going to prison for the bad things they did? Or can you have the child to kneel having a stone in each hand knocking the two over his or her head for doing bad things? I saw children got punished in that way, not because the father or the mother hated the child, but they wanted good for their children. We that have been taught this way are now seeing it was good for us. I told you before, a child left to his or her self can fall in to serious problem.

Don't leave them in the hall with the television on. Put off the television and send them to bed. Some kids have their own television in their bedrooms. You allow them this because you think that you love them. All I can say is wait and see what fruit that comes from their bedroom. You better find a way to lock it off when you want, because this good television can be looked upon as an object of sin. I like my television, but I don't let it carry me where it wants to. I control it, it doesn't control me, I listen to what I want. I watch what I want to watch. I brought it home, it didn't bring me home, I'm not its servant, it is my servant because I hold the control in my hand.

Some preachers teach a no law doctrine, but preach grace. They preach that when the Messiah died on the tree, he did away with the law the ten commandments. Nothing is faultier than this. The messiah never did away with Yahweh's laws, but came to show us how good keeping the law really is. There is nowhere in the bible one can find that saying to be true from Matthew 5:17-20. To those who believed that the law was done away with, this is what the messiah said; Think not that I came to destroy the law or the prophets. I came not to destroy, but to fulfil. For truly I say to you, to those again that believe that he put away the law at his death, till heaven and earth pass away, one youth or one title shall in no wise pass away from the law, till all things be accomplished. Verse 19 says; Whoever therefore shall break one! Not two, one of these least commandments, and shall do what? Shall teach men so, shall be called least in the kingdom of heaven, but whoever shall, shall do what? Whoever shall do and teach them, he shall be called great in the kingdom of heaven, for I say to you, that except your righteousness shall exceed the righteousness of the scribes and Pharisees, you shall in no wise enter the kingdom of heaven. The laws of Yahweh have never been done away nor will it ever be till heaven and earth pass away. Heaven is still here, also the earth. So, the laws of Yahweh are still binding.

Grace; they are preaching about grace, but grace is not there so that men can do whatever they please. Read the following scriptures to have a better understanding.

Romans 6:1-3; Romans 6:15-16, Romans 7:7-24; Romans 3:31. Then they go on to say the Sabbath has been done away with, it's for the Jews. Let me open you mind if you are one of those saying that. Did you know that Yahshua himself kept the Sabbath? Luke 4:31. Did you or did you not know that Yahshua the son of the most high, had been brought up in Nazareth? Read more about that in Luke 4:16 and Luke 6:1-3.

The Pharisees knew also about the keeping of the Sabbath. Know that they watched Yahshua to see if he would heal on the Sabbath that they might accuse him? Read Mark 3:1-4. They watched Yahshua, but they did not try to accuse him for keeping the Sabbath for they knew that it was right to keep the seven-day Sabbath and not the first day of the week. They watched him to see if he would heal on the Sabbath day. Since it was the Sabbath day, they thought to do healing was an offense. However, it was good for them to know that on the Sabbath day it is good to do well. Read Mark 6:1-2. After reading these scripture verses about the Sabbath, will you agree that the no law preachers take your mind away? Mark 7:6-7; Exodus 20:8-11. Now you may ask. Did Paul keep the Sabbath? And if he did, where can we find that he did in the bible? It is found in Acts 17:2; Acts 16:13.

Elohim himself kept the seventh day Sabbath. We can find that from Genesis 2:1-3. The seventh day is set apart for holy convocation. It is not like the six other days. For we are told to remember the seventh day to keep it holy. It also carries a preparation on Friday known as the sixth day. The women of the assemblies of Yahweh are all busy on Friday preparing the Sabbath meals, because no one should work on the Sabbath day.

The Sabbath starts from sunset Friday to sunset Saturday. It doesn't start from six to six as, so many people have said, or from midnight to midnight. Listen, don't we call half a day "mid-day" or "half day"? And do you know that half a night is called midnight or middle of the night? So why should anybody call it the start of a day or say that a day start at midnight? How could anyone say that?

Yahweh Elohim took the light from the darkness and Elohim called the light day, and the darkness he called night, so how could it be day and night at the same time? All the dark part is called night, and all the bright part is called day; Genesis 1:1. If you would like to know more about the creation, stop mistaking yourself follow the guide book: The Bible.

Are you an enemy of Yahweh? Try not to be.

I remember when I was about six years old there was at that time a plague, there were lots of mosquitoes, lots of bugs. The flees after it stung someone, it was very difficult to see it. They were small, but very troublesome They used to hide anywhere. In the bed, in clothes etc. They can jump very fast so that makes it difficult to kill them.

The bugs were also very troublesome. After it stung someone, it seeks a place to hide itself. In the bed, in the partition of the house, in clothes anywhere it finds a place. The mosquitoes do the same thing, all of them feed on people's blood. It was very easy to see or find them. These I remember seeing the bigger ones at home, using the candle to look for them. When we saw the mosquitoes, things were plenty in number. The people were unable to sleep. The smaller children cried because they got bitten by the mosquitoes very often. At times, we would put the lit candle on them and let them fall into the burning candle oil. The candles were the same we were using as light. We had to be very careful while using a candle. There was also a very small bug. This bug could not see. It lived in the ground. As children in those days, we used to play on the ground. After a few days, our fingers and toes were itching us not knowing the cause. Our mother or bigger sister would ask us to show them where we felt the itching, so we showed where we felt the itching. My mother would hold us to her, having a stretch pin or a needle. She dug our skin, fingers or toes to find what was causing the itching. Using the needle or pin in our flesh, she found some very small eggs that the bugs laid in our skin. When she pulled out the egg she found out of my or our flesh, there would be a hole in the flesh. From then on, we felt no pain. But if one egg is left, the pain would still be there. Just one egg could cause pain and if that one egg was not pulled out, more eggs would be laid under the skin. The funny thing is, we were seeing the eggs but what laid the eggs we could not see. Lots of children had this plague. Sometimes it laid so deep in the finger nail that to get it out, the parents had to cut the children nails. But only the eggs were seen not the bug. At that very moment, another type of small bug would be found in people's hair down to the root. Men, women, boy, girls, even babies were carrying that. Those who had that were always scratching their head. Sometimes they were seen on people's forehead going down on their faces.

Its eggs were just as those of the bugs. All these pests were laying eggs very fast. Some people used to cut their hair, the same way many are cutting their hair bald nowadays. When we found the bug eggs, we would put them on our kids thumb nail using the right thumb to kill them. They would make a bursting sound when we killed them.

As people, big and small, before there were good times and bad times. But through the help off the almighty some of us are still alive today. I love what I'm writing to you because it refreshes my memory.

Forgiving one another

I HAVE HEARD THAT MANY times in the past and I'm still hearing it even today. What is forgiveness, and how should we forgive one another? Now let us put it this way. If Jack and Jill said something to me and that which they said offended me very bad, and displeased me, I would say to them you all got me really mad. They saw that I was mad, so they came to me and said; forgive us please, we did not mean to get you offended with these words, forgive us please, we pray you. Should I say in reply, yes, I forgive you all but I'll never forget what you all said to me? My explanation is this; if you will forgive you must also forget. Today's time in which we live, many people are saying I forgive but I'll never forget. Even from church going people I heard that. Well since that is your way of forgiving, I have good news for you To forgive someone, you must also learn to forget. Matthew 6:9-15. You see the Bible have every help for man if we are willing to follow its guideline.

Ephesians 4:30-32, speaks about not grieving the Holy Spirit of Yahweh. It also says let all bitterness and wrath, and anger which you get, clamour and railing be put away from you in all malice, but to be kind one to another, tender-hearted, to love one as you love your own self; forgiving each other, even as Yahweh also in the messiah forgive you. If there is found in us bitterness, wrath, anger, clamour, railing and malice; those evil fruits of the flesh we will be unable to forgive others. So that is the reason why he says to put them away, get them out from you; and then you will be able to forgive and forget.

Now another one is to be found in Matthew 18:21-35. Get to your Bible and read. You see Peter was one who was always seeking asking questions. He always wanted to know, so he came to Yahshua and asked. How often his brother should forgive, Is it seven times? Yahshua answered. No Peter, not until seven times but until seventy times seven. Please do a little counting and go on reading to the very end of that chapter. Another one I would like you to read is Mark 12:28-34, you see, is not based on the church but Yahweh. If church will not do you good to help you with your salvation listen to what apostle Paul have to say to you. 2 Corinthians 6:17-18. Read and understand.

To you that doesn't have a bible, it says: Therefore, come out from among them, go, get out from among them because there is not truth in them, separate yourself from them. If you do that, Yahweh says he will receive you. Keep reading.

The invitation is for you. Come out from among these false preachers, leave out from there, and join his true body of believers. Take this call seriously and get out from these false churches religions.

Something else you might not know. Did you know that peter the apostle was hung upside down? I mean his head was hanging down and his feet were up. And while he was in that situation he told his wife to be strong, and that she should not give out her faith, but keep looking to Yahweh the author of their faith. So, this is how the life of Peter ended. But Yahshua, they nailed on the tree with nails in his hands and feet.

Eternal life to gain is not just faith, it takes more. It takes good making effort. There's always work to be done in keeping the commandment of Yahweh, such as to learn to forgive and to forget. John 3:16-21 and Psalm 139.

I do hope that you'll remember that this book was not written to put no one to shame, but that it will help you to gain stronger knowledge, especially those having families, husband and wives. Not forgetting how you ought to act; act wisely, strongly, manly, womanly; always ready to do good. Look to gain victory over Satan the devil. Don't let the devil take away your children. Look at them always, doing your best, your very best. And if there is what you cannot do, seek Yahweh's help. Thanks, and praises to all who read this book.

ALL PRAISES AND HONOR TO OUR HEAVENLY FATHER YAHWEH AND HIS SON YAHSHUA.

HALLELUYAH!!

THE END;

Printed in the United States
By Bookmasters